KB273358

혼공 중학 영문법 마스터

Level 2

혼공북스

이 책의 **구성과 특징**

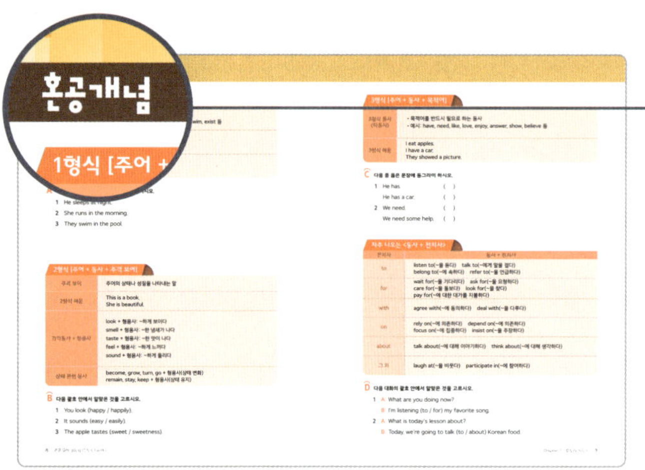

1 문법 개념 확인

문법 설명에서 꼭 배워야 할 핵심 내용을 도표로 정리했습니다. 각 개념을 배운 후에는 연계 문제를 통해 복습할 수 있습니다.

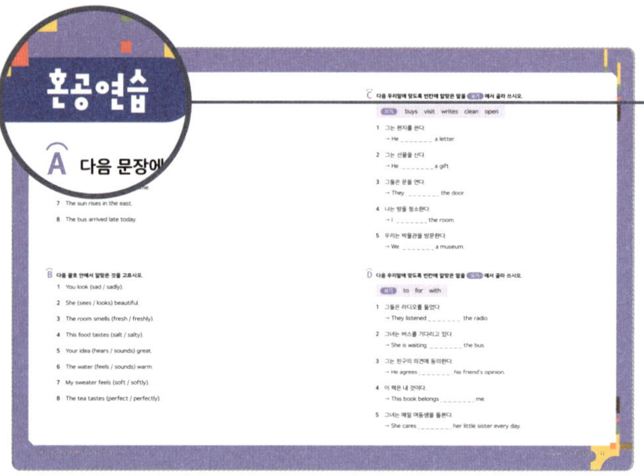

2 학습한 문법 내용 적용

'혼공개념'에서 학습한 문법에 대한 이해도를 점검할 수 있는 문제로 구성했습니다. 가장 기초적인 연습 문제를 통해 학습한 개념을 바로 확인해 볼 수 있습니다.

3 대표 기출 유형 연습

'혼공연습'에서 한 걸음 나아간 문제로 구성했습니다. 학습한 문법 개념들을 본격적으로 적용해 볼 수 있는 단계별 문제를 통해, 개념을 정확하게 이해할 수 있도록 구성했습니다.

4 서술형 평가 완성

서술형 평가에 대비할 수 있도록 빈칸에 알맞은 단어를 채우고, 문장을 영작할 수 있는 문제로 구성했습니다. 문법 개념을 이해하는 것뿐 아니라 쓰기에서도 활용하며 확실히 습득할 수 있습니다.

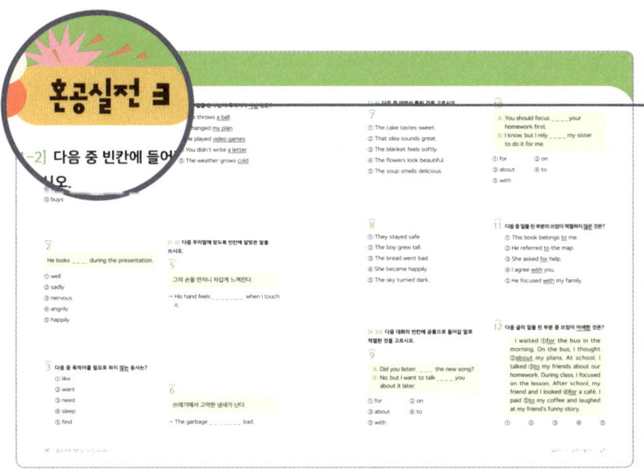

5 학교 시험 완벽 대비

각 챕터에서 배운 내용을 바탕으로 객관식, 주관식, 서술형, 독해 문제를 구성했습니다. 문제를 풀며 자신의 강점과 약점을 스스로 평가하고 학교 시험 실전 감각을 키울 수 있습니다.

400만 명의 수강생이 선택한 EBS 인기 강사 혼공쌤의 강의 32강을 무료로 수강할 수 있습니다.

유쾌한 혼공쌤의 강의를 통해 진정한 **중학 영문법 마스터**가 되어 보세요!

차례

1

문장의 형식 1

- 1형식 [주어 + 동사]
- 2형식 [주어 + 동사 + 주격 보어]
- 3형식 [주어 + 동사 + 목적어]
- 자주 나오는 <동사 + 전치사>

1형식 [주어 + 동사]

1형식 동사 (자동사)	• 목적어를 필요로 하지 않는 동사 • 예시: cry, live, go, run, laugh, leave, sleep, swim, exist 등
1형식 예문	The baby cries. He sleeps.
장소나 부사 추가 가능	She runs (in the park). They live (in a small village). He works (hard).

A 다음 문장에서 1형식 동사를 찾아 밑줄 치시오.

1 He sleeps at night.

2 She runs in the morning.

3 They swim in the pool.

2형식 [주어 + 동사 + 주격 보어]

주격 보어	주어의 상태나 성질을 나타내는 말
2형식 예문	This is a book. She is beautiful.
감각동사 + 형용사	look + 형용사: ~하게 보이다 smell + 형용사: ~한 냄새가 나다 taste + 형용사: ~한 맛이 나다 feel + 형용사: ~하게 느끼다 sound + 형용사: ~하게 들리다
상태 관련 동사	become, grow, turn, go + 형용사(상태 변화) remain, stay, keep + 형용사(상태 유지)

B 다음 괄호 안에서 알맞은 것을 고르시오.

1 You look (happy / happily).

2 It sounds (easy / easily).

3 The apple tastes (sweet / sweetness).

<table>
<tr><td colspan="2">3형식 [주어 + 동사 + 목적어]</td></tr>
<tr><td>3형식 동사
(타동사)</td><td>• 목적어를 반드시 필요로 하는 동사
• 예시: have, need, like, love, enjoy, answer, show, believe 등</td></tr>
<tr><td>3형식 예문</td><td>I eat apples.
I have a car.
They showed a picture.</td></tr>
</table>

C 다음 중 옳은 문장에 동그라미 하시오.

1 He has.　　　　　(　)

　 He has a car.　　　(　)

2 We need.　　　　(　)

　 We need some help.　(　)

자주 나오는 ⟨동사 + 전치사⟩

전치사	동사 + 전치사
to	listen to(~을 듣다)　talk to(~에게 말을 걸다) belong to(~에 속하다)　refer to(~을 언급하다)
for	wait for(~을 기다리다)　ask for(~을 요청하다) care for(~을 돌보다)　look for(~을 찾다) pay for(~에 대한 대가를 지불하다)
with	agree with(~에 동의하다)　deal with(~을 다루다)
on	rely on(~에 의존하다)　depend on(~에 의존하다) focus on(~에 집중하다)　insist on(~을 주장하다)
about	talk about(~에 대해 이야기하다)　think about(~에 대해 생각하다)
그 외	laugh at(~을 비웃다)　participate in(~에 참여하다)

D 다음 대화의 괄호 안에서 알맞은 것을 고르시오.

1 A: What are you doing now?

　 B: I'm listening (to / for) my favorite song.

2 A: What is today's lesson about?

　 B: Today, we're going to talk (to / about) Korean food.

A 다음 문장에서 1형식 동사를 찾아 밑줄 치시오.

1 The baby cried.

2 Birds fly in the sky.

3 The kids laugh together.

4 The stars twinkle at night.

5 She walks to school.

6 The phone rang for a long time.

7 The sun rises in the east.

8 The bus arrived late today.

B 다음 괄호 안에서 알맞은 것을 고르시오.

1 You look (sad / sadly).

2 She (sees / looks) beautiful.

3 The room smells (fresh / freshly).

4 This food tastes (salt / salty).

5 Your idea (hears / sounds) great.

6 The water (feels / sounds) warm.

7 My sweater feels (soft / softly).

8 The tea tastes (perfect / perfectly).

C 다음 우리말에 맞도록 빈칸에 알맞은 말을 보기 에서 골라 쓰시오.

> 보기 buys   visit   writes   clean   open

1 그는 편지를 쓴다.

→ He ___________ a letter.

2 그는 선물을 산다.

→ He ___________ a gift.

3 그들은 문을 연다.

→ They ___________ the door.

4 나는 방을 청소한다.

→ I ___________ the room.

5 우리는 박물관을 방문한다.

→ We ___________ a museum.

D 다음 우리말에 맞도록 빈칸에 알맞은 말을 보기 에서 골라 쓰시오.

> 보기 to   for   with

1 그들은 라디오를 들었다.

→ They listened ___________ the radio.

2 그녀는 버스를 기다리고 있다.

→ She is waiting ___________ the bus.

3 그는 친구의 의견에 동의한다.

→ He agrees ___________ his friend's opinion.

4 이 책은 내 것이다.

→ This book belongs ___________ me.

5 그녀는 매일 여동생을 돌본다.

→ She cares ___________ her little sister every day.

A 다음 문장에서 1형식 동사를 찾아 밑줄 치시오.

1   It rains.

2   Cats jump.

3   Water flows.

4   The sun sets.

5   Fish swim.

6   The clock ticks.

7   The bell rings.

8   The car stops.

9   The wind blows.

10   The flower blooms.

11   Birds sing on the tree.

12   Noel jogs every morning.

13   They exercise in the evening.

14   The store opens at 9 a.m.

15   He dances all night.

16   He left in the morning.

17   She stayed with her friends.

18   She moved slowly.

19   They arrived safely.

20   The sun shines brightly.

1   He (sees / looks) smart.

2   The baby (looks / watches) healthy.

3   It (listens / sounds) great.

4   That (hears / sounds) wonderful.

5   This place looks (peace / peaceful).

6   The sky looks (clear / clearly).

7   She looks (strong / strongly).

8   The room smells (bad / badly).

9   This food smells (strange / strangely).

10   The soup smells (delicious / deliciously).

11   The garbage smells (terrible / terribly).

12   The cake tastes (sweet / sweetly).

13   The ice cream tastes (nice / nicely).

14   This juice tastes (sour / sourly).

15   This curry tastes (spicy / spice).

16   The jacket feels too (loose / loosely) on me.

17   The sand feels (hot / hotly) under my feet.

18   This chair feels (uncomfortable / uncomfortably).

19   He feels (nervous / nervously) before the test.

20   This topic sounds (important / importantly).

C 다음 괄호 안에서 알맞은 것을 고르시오.

1   He became (angry / angrily).

2   She became (famous / famously).

3   We became (rich / richly).

4   The snow became (heavy / heavily).

5   The sky grows (dark / darkly).

6   The weather grew (warm / warmly).

7   The wind grew (strong / strongly).

8   The fire grew (weak / weakly) in the cold wind.

9   The air grows (cold / coldly) as the sun sets.

10   Her voice grew (soft / softly) as she spoke to the baby.

11   Her face turned (red / redly).

12   The milk turned (sour / sourly).

13   The water turned (clear / clearly).

14   The air turned (fresh / freshly).

15   I told my friend to stay (calm / calmly).

16   The dog will stay (health / healthy).

17   The road will stay (wet / wetness) after the rain.

18   I hope you stay (happy / happily).

19   You must keep (quiet / quitely).

20   He promised to remain (honest / honestly).

 다음 대화의 괄호 안에서 알맞은 것을 고르시오.

1 A: Can you care (for / with) my dog today?
   B: Yes, I can.

2 A: What are you doing?
   B: I'm trying to look (to / for) my phone.

3 A: What kind of music do you listen (to / with)?
   B: I love classical music.

4 A: Does this book belong (to / for) you?
   B: No, it doesn't.

5 A: Did you think (to / about) the menu for lunch?
   B: Yes, I want bulgogi.

6 A: How do you deal (on / with) stress?
   B: I usually take a walk.

7 A: Did you ask (on / for) help with your homework?
   B: No, I didn't need any help this time.

8 A: You need to focus (on / with) your homework.
   B: Okay, I will.

9 A: Does the team's success depend (to / on) the coach?
   B: Yes, it really does.

10 A: Are we going to wait (to / for) the bus here?
    B: Yes, let's wait here.

A 다음 우리말에 맞도록 빈칸에 알맞은 말을 쓰시오.

1 그들은 일한다.
→ They ____________.

2 우리는 잔다.
→ We ____________.

3 기차가 움직인다.
→ The train ____________.

4 그녀가 춤춘다.
→ She ____________.

5 그는 걷는다.
→ He ____________.

6 새들이 아침에 노래한다.
→ The birds ____________ in the morning.

7 해가 서쪽으로 진다.
→ The sun ____________ in the west.

8 기차가 역에 멈춘다.
→ The train ____________ at the station.

9 그는 언덕 위로 달린다.
→ He ____________ up the hill.

10 개는 강에서 수영을 한다.
→ The dog ____________ in the river.

11 아이들이 크게 웃는다.
→ The kids ____________ loudly.

12 버스가 제시간에 도착한다.
→ The bus ____________ on time.

1 그 병은 비어 보인다.

→ The bottle ____________ empty.

2 생선에서 좋지 못한 냄새가 난다.

→ The fish ____________ bad.

3 수프가 너무 짠 맛이 난다.

→ The soup ____________ too salty.

4 침대가 아늑하게 느껴진다.

→ The bed ____________ cozy.

5 그 농담은 웃기게 들린다.

› The joke ____________ funny.

6 도로가 안전해 보인다.

→ The road ____________ safe.

7 쿠키가 달콤한 맛이 난다.

→ The cookie ____________ sweet.

8 수프에서 그윽한 냄새가 난다.

→ The soup ____________ rich.

9 꽃들에게서 좋은 냄새가 난다.

→ The flowers ____________ good.

10 얼음이 차갑게 느껴진다.

→ The ice ____________ cold.

11 하늘이 흐려 보인다.

→ The sky ____________ cloudy.

12 기계 소리가 시끄럽게 들린다.

→ The machine ____________ noisy.

C 다음 괄호 안의 단어들을 바르게 배열하시오.

1 (looks / the water / clear / .)
→

2 (sleepy / the baby / looks / .)
→

3 (feels / the blanket / warm / .)
→

4 (sounds / the plan / great / .)
→

5 (tastes / sweet / the chocolate / .)
→

6 (looks / quiet / the library / .)
→

7 (red / turned / his face / .)
→

8 (stayed / I / awake / all night / .)
→

9 (keep / need to / healthy / we / .)
→

10 (the milk / bad / went / .)
→

11 (turned / yellow / the leaves / .)
→

12 (strong / he / grew / after exercise / .)
→

13 (turned / the sky / gray / before the rain / .)
→

14 (stayed / the room / warm / all night / .)
→

15 (she / nervous / became / before the interview / .)
→

1 (listens / he / my / to / advice / .)

   →

2 (to / talks / she / her / parents / .)

   →

3 (belongs / me / to / this eraser / .)

   →

4 (waited / he / the bus / for / for 10 minutes / .)

   →

5 (she / asked / some help / for / .)

   →

6 (am / I / for / looking / my textbook / .)

   →

7 (for / paid / he / the snacks / at the store / .)

   →

8 (didn't / she / with / agree / the new rules / .)

   →

9 (relies / she / on / for information / the internet / .)

   →

10 (is / she / focusing / her essay / on / .)

   →

11 (laughed / at / they / the funny joke / .)

   →

12 (participated / the group study / she / in / .)

   →

13 (for / she / cares / her little brother / after school / .)

   →

14 (deal / you / should / with / your stress / .)

   →

15 (they / on / insist / their opinion / .)

   →

[1-2] 다음 중 빈칸에 들어갈 말로 가장 적절한 것을 고르시오.

1

> She _______ in a big city.

① lives
② brings
③ has
④ shows
⑤ buys

2

> He looks _______ during the presentation.

① well
② sadly
③ nervous
④ angrily
⑤ happily

3 다음 중 목적어를 필요로 하지 <u>않는</u> 동사는?

① like
② want
③ need
④ sleep
⑤ find

4 다음 중 밑줄 친 부분이 목적어가 <u>아닌</u> 것은?

① She throws <u>a ball</u>.
② I changed <u>my plan</u>.
③ He played <u>video games</u>.
④ You didn't write <u>a letter</u>.
⑤ The weather grows <u>cold</u>.

[5-6] 다음 우리말에 맞도록 빈칸에 알맞은 말을 쓰시오.

5

> 그의 손을 만지니 차갑게 느껴진다.

→ His hand feels ____________ when I touch it.

6

> 쓰레기에서 고약한 냄새가 난다.

→ The garbage ____________ bad.

7

① The cake tastes sweet.

② That idea sounds great.

③ The blanket feels softly.

④ The flowers look beautiful.

⑤ The soup smells delicious.

8

① They stayed safe.

② The boy grew tall.

③ The bread went bad.

④ She became happily.

⑤ The sky turned dark.

[9-10] 다음 대화의 빈칸에 공통으로 들어갈 말로
적절한 것을 고르시오.

9

A: Did you listen ______ the new song?
B: No, but I want to talk ______ you
about it later.

① for   ② on

③ about   ④ to

⑤ with

10

A: You should focus ______ your
homework first.
B: I know, but I rely ______ my sister
to do it for me.

① for   ② on

③ about   ④ to

⑤ with

11 다음 중 밑줄 친 부분의 쓰임이 적절하지 <u>않은</u> 것은?

① This book belongs <u>to</u> me.

② He referred <u>to</u> the map.

③ She asked <u>for</u> help.

④ I agree <u>with</u> you.

⑤ He focused <u>with</u> my family.

12 다음 글의 밑줄 친 부분 중 쓰임이 <u>어색한</u> 것은?

I waited ①<u>for</u> the bus in the morning. On the bus, I thought ②<u>about</u> my plans. At school, I talked ③<u>to</u> my friends about our homework. During class, I focused on the lesson. After school, my friend and I looked ④<u>for</u> a café. I paid ⑤<u>to</u> my coffee and laughed at my friend's funny story.

①   ②   ③   ④   ⑤

[13-14] **다음 문장에서 어법상 틀린 곳을 찾아 바르게 고치시오.**

13

This sweater feels warmly and cozy.

___________ → ___________

14

Your idea sounds perfectly for this project.

___________ → ___________

15 다음 대화의 빈칸에 들어갈 말로 가장 적절한 것은?

A: Did you see the tree?
B: Yes, it _______ red.

① controlled
② opened
③ turned
④ knew
⑤ lived

[16-17] **다음 우리말에 맞도록 괄호 안의 단어들을 바르게 배열하시오.**

16

여러분의 손을 씻고 건강을 유지하세요.
(hands / wash / and / healthy / your / stay / .)

→ ___________________________

17

그 가게는 내일까지 열려 있을 것이다.
(the shop / remain / will / open / tomorrow / until / .)

→ ___________________________

18 다음 중 빈칸에 들어갈 말로 적절하지 <u>않은</u> 것은?

After the rain, the sky ___________ clear and blue.

① became
② grew
③ turned
④ had
⑤ went

[19-20] 다음 우리말에 맞도록 빈칸에 알맞은 말을 보기 에서 골라 쓰시오.

보기   on   for   with   to   about

19

너는 그녀의 의견에 동의하니?

→ Do you agree __________ her opinion?

20

그녀는 자신의 권리를 주장한다.

→ She insists __________ her rights.

21 다음 대화에서 어법상 틀린 곳을 찾아 바르게 고치시오.

A: Are you going to participate the school festival?
B: Yes, I'll join the singing contest.

__________ → __________

22 다음 두 대화의 빈칸에 들어갈 말이 바르게 짝지어진 것은?

• A: The cookies smell _______!
  Did you bake them yourself?
  B: Yes, I did.
• A: You look upset. Are you okay?
  B: I'm trying to _______ positive, but it's hard.

① delicious – stay
② delicious – need
③ delicious – love
④ deliciously – have
⑤ deliciously – change

23 다음 글의 밑줄 친 부분 중 어법상 옳은 것끼리 바르게 짝지어진 것은?

My friend and I went to the park. The flowers smelled ⓐwonderfully. The lake looked so ⓑpeaceful under the sunlight. We sat on a bench. It felt warm and ⓒcomfortably. Everything around us sounded ⓓcalm and relaxing. The breeze felt ⓔcool on our faces.

① ⓐ, ⓑ
② ⓑ, ⓒ
③ ⓑ, ⓓ
④ ⓐ, ⓒ, ⓔ
⑤ ⓑ, ⓓ, ⓔ

2

문장의 형식 2

- 4형식
  [주어 + 동사 + 간접목적어 + 직접목적어]
- 4형식에서 3형식으로 전환
- 5형식
  [주어 + 동사 + 목적어 + 목적격 보어]
- 5형식: 사역동사와 지각동사
  [주어 + 지각 / 사역동사 + 목적어
  + 동사원형]

4형식 [주어 + 동사 + 간접목적어 + 직접목적어]

4형식 동사 (수여동사)	give, show, send, tell, teach, buy, make, lend, offer, cook 등
간접목적어 (~에게)	me, you, him, her, us, them, it 등
직접목적어 (~을 / 를)	목적어(~을 / 를)에 해당하는 모든 명사 예문: I gave her a letter. 수여동사 간접목적어 직접목적어

A 다음 문장에서 간접목적어를 찾아 밑줄 치시오.

1 I gave him a book.

2 He showed us his new car.

3 My mom made me a sandwich.

4형식에서 3형식으로 전환

형식	주어 + 동사 + 간접목적어 + 직접목적어 (4형식) 주어 + 동사 + 직접목적어 + to / for / of + 간접목적어 (3형식)
3형식 예문	I gave a gift to her.
to를 쓰는 동사	give, send, lend, pass, show, tell, bring, write, offer, teach, hand, read 등
for를 쓰는 동사	make, buy, cook, get, find, build 등
of를 쓰는 동사	ask, require 등

B 다음 괄호 안에서 알맞은 것을 고르시오.

1 I sent a letter (to / for) him.

2 He buys some flowers (to / for) his mother.

3 She asked a question (on / of) the speaker.

5형식 [주어 + 동사 + 목적어 + 목적격 보어]

목적격 보어	목적어를 보충 설명하거나 목적어의 상태를 나타내는 말	
목적격 보어의 형태	**동사**	**목적격 보어**
	call, name, make 등	명사
	make, keep, find 등	형용사
	ask, want, tell, advise, allow, enable, order, encourage 등	to 부정사
5형식 예문	He called her a genius. The news made me happy. I encouraged him to study hard.	

C 다음 중 밑줄 친 목적격 보어의 형태가 옳으면 ○, 틀리면 X를 표시하시오.

1 We called her <u>a hero</u>. ( )

2 We makc our parents <u>proudly</u>. ( )

3 I encouraged him <u>trying</u> again. ( )

5형식: 사역동사와 지각동사 [주어 + 지각 / 사역동사 + 목적어 + 동사원형]

구분	사역동사	지각동사
주요 동사	make, have, let	see, watch, hear, feel 등
의미	~가 …하게 하다	~가 …하는 것을 보다, 듣다, 느끼다 등
예문	She made him cry. I let him go home early.	She heard him sing a song. He felt the wind blow.
		I saw him running in the park. *진행의 뜻이 강조될 때 현재분사(-ing)를 씀

D 다음 대화의 괄호 안에서 알맞은 것을 고르시오.

1 A: What are you doing now?

   B: I am making students (prepare / to prepare) for the test.

2 A: Why are you so surprised?

   B: I saw a bird (fly / to fly) into the room.

A 다음 괄호 안에서 알맞은 것을 고르시오.

1 She gave (I / me) a pen.

2 They told (she / her) a story.

3 I taught (he / him) English.

4 He made (we / us) coffee.

5 We showed (they / them) his photo.

6 He offered (you / your) some water.

7 I bought (her / hers) a bag.

8 They brought (his / him) a towel.

B 다음 괄호 안에서 알맞은 것을 고르시오.

1 I gave a pen (to / for) my teacher.

2 He sent an email (to / for) his boss.

3 They made breakfast (to / for) their neighbors.

4 He cooked dinner (to / for) his family.

5 She showed the recipe (to / for) her classmates.

6 They bought a toy (to / for) the baby.

7 They built a sandcastle (to / for) their kids.

8 We asked questions (in / of) the students.

C 다음 우리말에 맞도록 빈칸에 알맞은 말을 보기 에서 골라 쓰시오.

보기   him   dark   named   to help us   warm   to study

1   우리는 그 개를 Max라고 이름을 지었다.
→ We ________________ the dog Max.

2   그녀는 그를 리더로 만들었다.
→ She made ________________ the leader.

3   나는 내 손을 따뜻하게 유지했다.
→ I kept my hands ________________.

4   그들은 방이 어둡다는 것을 알게 되었다.
→ They found the room ________________.

5   나는 그가 공부하기를 원한다.
→ I want him ________________.

6   우리는 그녀에게 우리를 도와달라고 요청했다.
→ We asked her ________________.

D 다음 문장의 밑줄 친 부분을 알맞은 형태로 바꿔 쓰시오.

1   My mom made me <u>to clean</u> my room.   → ________________

2   He let me <u>playing</u> games for an hour.   → ________________

3   The teacher had us <u>to practice</u> a lot.   → ________________

4   They saw the cat <u>to climb</u> the tree.   → ________________

5   I heard the dog <u>to bark</u> outside.   → ________________

A 다음 괄호 안에서 알맞은 것을 고르시오.

1 He (took / gave) me a book.

2 She (told / heard) him a secret.

3 They (showed / watched) us a new dress.

4 She (sent / listened) her friend a message.

5 My mom (ate / cooked) us dinner.

6 Tom (saw / bought) me new shoes.

7 I (lent / took) his friend my bike.

8 Grandma (made / created) me a warm sweater.

9 They (offered / produced) him a job.

10 He gave (they / them) a surprise gift.

11 They lent (you / your) some money.

12 He showed (she / her) his project.

13 She told (his / him) the new plan.

14 She made (I / me) a beautiful card.

15 He taught (they / them) English.

16 He sent (we / us) an invitation card.

17 I bought (her / she) a new pencil case.

18 He told (they / them) the truth.

19 She made (we / us) a fruit salad.

20 The teacher taught (him / his) a new lesson.

1   I gave a pencil (to / for) my friend.

2   She wrote a letter (to / of) her teacher.

3   He sent flowers (to / of) his mom.

4   We made toys (to / for) the kids.

5   He handed a note (to / for) me.

6   He bought a book (to / for) his girlfriend.

7   They built a house (to / for) people.

8   She showed rings (to / for) her parents.

9   He told a joke (to / for) his friends.

10   I asked a question (in / of) the leader.

11   She made a necklace (to / for) her sister.

12   I cooked lunch (to / for) children.

13   He taught Korean (to / for) students.

14   They offered advice (to / for) their neighbor.

15   The teacher required homework (to / of) the students.

16   She bought a robot (to / for) her little brother.

17   They built a doghouse (to / for) their puppy.

18   The chef made dessert (to / for) the customers.

19   I lent my headphones (to / for) my roommate.

20   He handed the documents (to / for) the officer.

C 다음 괄호 안에서 알맞은 것을 고르시오.

1 They (called / described) him a superhero.

2 She (named / spoke) her dog Lucky.

3 We (made / built) her the leader of the group.

4 I (found / knew) the room clean.

5 She (kept / planted) the garden beautiful.

6 He (allowed / explained) his dog to run freely.

7 She (said / told) her brother to clean the room.

8 He (advised / mentioned) his friend to study harder.

9 We (encouraged / loved) them to join the competition.

10 He (ordered / explained) the workers to fix the machine.

11 I (owned / found) the problem simple.

12 She (made / introduced) the meeting a success.

13 He (asked / liked) the waiter to bring more water.

14 The teacher (wanted / suggested) the children to focus.

15 They (kept / waited) the environment safe.

16 We (made / went) the trip an adventure.

17 I (found / understanded) the test easy.

18 They (knew / made) the lesson enjoyable.

19 The teacher (ordered / explained) the students to sit quietly.

20 The manager (enabled / worked) the team to achieve their goals.

1   A: My parents let me (go / to go) to the concert last night.
    B: That sounds good.

2   A: Did you hear her (sing / to sing) at the talent show?
    B: Yes, she was great.

3   A: My mom made me (clean / to clean) my room.
    B: That's a good thing.

4   A: My dad let me (play / playing) video games after dinner.
    B: That's nice.

5   A: I watched her (drawing / to draw) a picture in class.
    B: She's good at drawing.

6   A: I saw dogs (wag / to wag) their tails in the park.
    B: Me, too. They looked so happy!

7   A: I watched him (play / to play) soccer.
    B: He's really good at playing soccer.

8   A: The teacher had us (leave / to leave) early today.
    B: That's lucky.

9   A: I felt the wind (blow / to blow) really hard.
    B: I know. It felt like a storm was coming.

10 A: My coach made me (run / to run) five laps.
    B: That sounds exhausting.

A 다음 우리말에 맞도록 빈칸에 알맞은 말을 쓰시오.

1 그는 나에게 공책을 주었다.

→ He ___________ me a notebook.

2 나는 그에게 책을 사 주었다.

→ I ___________ him a book.

3 우리는 선생님께 질문했다.

→ We ___________ the teacher a question.

4 우리는 그녀에게 생일 카드를 보냈다.

→ We ___________ her a birthday card.

5 그는 나에게 돈을 좀 빌려주었다.

→ He ___________ me some money.

6 나는 그녀에게 내 사진을 보여 주었다.

→ I ___________ her my picture.

7 나는 아이들에게 이야기를 읽어 주었다.

→ I ___________ the children a story.

8 그녀는 나에게 간식을 좀 가져다주었다.

→ She ___________ me some snacks.

9 나는 그들에게 도움을 좀 제공했다.

→ I ___________ them some help.

10 우리는 그들에게 선물을 보냈다.

→ We ___________ them a present.

11 그녀는 우리에게 중요한 정보를 주었다.

→ She ___________ us important information.

12 엄마가 나에게 맛있는 음식을 좀 만들어 주셨다.

→ Mom ___________ me some delicious food.

1 그는 나에게 좋은 조언을 해 주었다.

   → He gave good advice ___________ me.

2 나는 그녀에게 내 전화기를 보여 주었다.

   → I showed my phone ___________ her.

3 그녀는 친구에게 커피를 만들어 주었다.

   → She made coffee ___________ her friend.

4 나는 노인분께 내 좌석을 양보했다.

   → I offered my seat ___________ the elderly man.

5 우리는 그녀에게 차를 사 주었다.

   → We bought a car ___________ her.

6 나는 그에게 내 열쇠를 빌려주었다.

   → I lent my key ___________ him.

7 나는 그녀에게 공을 패스했다.

   → I passed the ball ___________ her.

8 우리는 아이들에게 음료수를 가져다주었다.

   → We brought drinks ___________ the kids.

9 우리는 그녀에게 저녁 식사를 만들어 주었다.

   → We cooked dinner ___________ her.

10 우리는 선생님께 도움을 요청했다.

   → We asked a favor ___________ the teacher.

11 그는 나에게 그의 전화번호를 알려 주었다.

   → He told his phone number ___________ me.

12 그녀는 나에게 피아노를 가르쳐 주었다.

   → She taught piano ___________ me.

C 다음 괄호 안의 단어들을 바르게 배열하시오.

1 (Lucy / named / her doll / she / .)

→ ________________________________

2 (he / the soup / made / tasty / .)

→ ________________________________

3 (we / the door / kept / open / .)

→ ________________________________

4 (want / to join the team / we / her / .)

→ ________________________________

5 (kept / they / the baby / quiet / .)

→ ________________________________

6 (made / we / the house / warm / .)

→ ________________________________

7 (called / people / a success / the invention / .)

→ ________________________________

8 (I / him / to open the window / asked / .)

→ ________________________________

9 (ordered / they / to move forward / the soldiers / .)

→ ________________________________

10 (advised / to take a break / I / her / .)

→ ________________________________

11 (told / to write again / the teacher / us / .)

→ ________________________________

12 (allowed / she / me / to go to the party / .)

→ ________________________________

13 (encouraged / we / the children / to play outside / .)

→ ________________________________

14 (she / to finish the project / ordered / him / .)

→ ________________________________

15 (I / this city / very beautiful / found / .)

→ ________________________________

 다음 괄호 안의 단어들을 바르게 배열하시오.

1 (we / a cat / saw / sleep / .)

→ ____

2 (cry / made / the movie / us / .)

→ ____

3 (saw / the teacher / us / write the answers / .)

→ ____

4 (take a short break / let / the coach / us / .)

→ ____

5 (felt / we / the car / move / .)

→ ____

6 (play soccer / watched / she / her brother / .)

→ ____

7 (I / my friend / study English / had / .)

→ ____

8 (made / stay inside / the rain / us / .)

→ ____

9 (I / my sister / sing in her room / heard / .)

→ ____

10 (saw / the bus / leave the station / we / .)

→ ____

11 (she / her friend / let / borrow her book / .)

→ ____

12 (I / someone / knock on the door / heard / .)

→ ____

13 (watched / we / her / reading a book / .)

→ ____

14 (had / the manager / us / arrange the chairs / .)

→ ____

15 (watched / the children / we / play in the park / .)

→ ____

1 다음 중 밑줄 친 부분이 어법상 **틀린** 것은?

① He gave <u>me</u> a laptop.

② She sent <u>him</u> an email.

③ He showed <u>we</u> his picture.

④ I bought <u>my brother</u> a toy.

⑤ I lent <u>my friend</u> some money.

[2-4] 다음 중 빈칸에 들어갈 말로 가장 적절한 것을 고르시오.

2

She gave __________ a birthday gift.

① he
② to he
③ to him
④ his
⑤ him

3

The teacher allowed us __________.

① talk
② to talk
③ talking
④ to talking
⑤ talks

4

The teacher made the class __________.

① laugh
② is laughing
③ to laugh
④ was laughing
⑤ will laugh

[5-6] 다음 우리말에 맞도록 빈칸에 들어갈 말로 가장 적절한 것을 고르시오.

5

• 나는 누군가가 도서관에서 노래를 흥얼거리고 있는 것을 들었다.
→ I __________ someone humming a song in the library.

① saw
② felt
③ smelled
④ heard
⑤ watched

6

• 그녀는 운전자가 속도를 줄이게 했다.
→ She __________ the driver slow down.

① told
② got
③ made
④ ordered
⑤ asked

7 다음 대화의 빈칸에 공통으로 들어갈 말로 가장 적절한 것은?

> A: Can you show the photo _______ me?
> B: Sure, I'll send it _______ you now.

① for   ② on
③ about   ④ to
⑤ of

[8-10] 다음 우리말에 맞도록 빈칸에 알맞은 한 단어를 쓰시오.

8

> 저를 소개합니다.

→ Let me _______________ myself.

9

> 그녀는 학생들이 그 문장을 쓰게 했다.

→ She had the students _______________ the sentence.

10

> 우리는 그녀가 야구팀에 가입하도록 격려했다.

→ We encouraged her _______________ join the baseball team.

11 다음 중 밑줄 친 부분이 어법상 **틀린** 것은?

① I made the kids <u>stop</u> fighting.

② I had him apo<u>logize</u> for his fault.

③ He let his friend <u>use</u> his laptop.

④ He wanted the teacher <u>explain</u> it again.

⑤ She saw the car <u>turn</u> left at the corner.

12 다음 글의 밑줄 친 부분 중 어법상 **틀린** 곳은?

> I was busy yesterday. I ①<u>gave</u> my friend a book for her birthday. Then, I ②<u>bought</u> my brother a pen for his exam. At lunch, I ③<u>said</u> my classmates a funny story. Later, I ④<u>made</u> my sister a snack because she was hungry. In the evening, I ⑤<u>offered</u> my neighbor some cookies.

①   ②   ③   ④   ⑤

[13-15] 다음 문장에서 어법상 <u>틀린</u> 곳을 찾아 바르게 고치시오.

13

The music made people dancing.

___________ → ___________

14

The parents enabled their daughter learn the piano.

___________ → ___________

15

Your idea sounds perfectly for this project.

___________ → ___________

[16-17] 다음 중 빈칸에 들어갈 말로 적절하지 <u>않은</u> 것을 고르시오.

16

The teacher _______ me the book.

① had
② gave
③ sent
④ bought
⑤ showed

17

I _______ him study in the room.

① made
② had
③ let
④ saw
⑤ want

18 다음 우리말에 맞도록 괄호 안의 단어를 이용하여 빈칸에 알맞은 말을 쓰시오.

어머니는 내가 그녀의 핸드폰을 빌리는 것을 허락하셨다. (borrow)

→ My mother allowed me ________________ her phone.

19

- A: I made a cake _______ you.
  B: Wow, thank you.
- A: I bought a sweater _______ my dad.
  B: Oh, that's nice. I'm sure he'll like it.

① for   ② to
③ about   ④ of
⑤ with

20

- A: I will ask him _______ the festival.
  B: That's a good idea.
- A: My parents allowed me _______ the
    meeting tonight.
  B: That's great!

① attend   ② attends
③ to attend   ④ attending
⑤ to attending

[21-22] 다음 우리말에 맞도록 괄호 안의 단어들을
바르게 배열하시오.

21

의사는 내가 며칠 동안 쉬게 했다.
(the doctor / me / made / rest /
for a few days / .)

→ ____________________________________

22

내 아들은 그들이 노인을 돕고 있는 것을 보았다.
(helping / them / saw / my son / an
elderly man / .)

→ ____________________________________

23 다음 글의 밑줄 친 부분 중 어법상 옳은 것끼리
바르게 짝지어진 것은?

A farmer lived in a small village with his family. One day, his family didn't have enough food. He wanted his family ⓐto have more to eat. He asked his children ⓑhelp dig the ground and plant seeds. The farmer ⓒmade his animals eat the old grass. He believed their hard work would make the plants ⓓto grow. Soon, the fields were full of food, and his family was happy.

① ⓐ, ⓑ
② ⓐ, ⓒ
③ ⓑ, ⓓ
④ ⓐ, ⓒ, ⓓ
⑤ ⓑ, ⓒ, ⓓ

3

형용사와 부사

- 형용사의 쓰임
- 수와 양을 나타내는 형용사
- 부사의 쓰임
- 빈도부사와 주의해야 할 부사

형용사의 쓰임

형태	happy, sunny, tall, big, good 등 -able, -ial, -ible, -ic, -ive, -ous, -ful 등 lovely, friendly, costly, lively, timely, elderly 등
명사 앞 수식	예시: **beautiful** flowers
보어 역할	예문: She is **happy**.
대명사 뒤 수식	-thing, -body, -one + 형용사 예시: something **special** (○), **special** something (X)

A 다음 문장에서 형용사를 찾아 밑줄 치시오.

1 I have a new phone.

2 The sky is cloudy.

3 She gave me something good.

수와 양을 나타내는 형용사

많은 many much a lot(lots) of	many	+ 셀 수 있는 명사
	much	+ 셀 수 없는 명사
	a lot(lots) of	+ 둘 다 가능
	예문: **A lot of** books are on the table.	
조금의 a few a little 거의 없는 few little	a few	+ 복수명사
	a little	+ 셀 수 없는 명사
	few	+ 복수명사
	little	+ 셀 수 없는 명사
	예문: **A few** students are reading books. They have **little** food to eat.	

B 다음 괄호 안에서 알맞은 것을 고르시오.

1 She has (many / much) friends.

2 There are (a few / a little) apples.

3 He drank (few / little) water.

형태	형용사 + ly	happy - happily quick - quickly clear - clearly loud - loudly
	형용사와 형태가 같은 부사	fast, hard, late(lately: 최근에), high(highly: 매우, 크게), early, near 등
	그 외	so, too, very, rather, pretty, quite, well 등
역할	동사 수식	He laughed **loudly**.
	형용사 수식	She is **very** happy.
	다른 부사 수식	You drove **too** fast.
	문장 전체 수식	**Surprisingly**, the test was very easy.

C 다음 문장에서 부사를 찾아 밑줄 치시오.

1 We danced happily.

2 Clearly, we made a mistake.

3 The internet is too slow.

	be동사, 조동사 뒤 또는 일반동사 앞에 사용	
빈도부사	발생 횟수 always > usually > often > sometimes > hardly, rarely > never 예문: She always wakes up early. He never forgets my birthday.	
주의해야 할 부사	too(또한, 역시) - 긍정문 I like music. She likes music, too.	either(또한, 역시) - 부정문 I don't like bread. Sam doesn't like bread, either.
	very(매우, 아주) - 형용사, 부사 수식 He runs **very** fast.	
	well(잘, 제대로) - 형용사는 good He speaks Korean **well**.	

C 다음 대화의 괄호 안에서 알맞은 것을 고르시오.

1 A: What does he like to do?

B: He (always likes / likes always) to play soccer.

2 A: What is she good at?

B: She cooks (good / well).

A 다음 문장에서 형용사를 찾아 밑줄 치시오.

1   The coffee is hot.

2   I want a new book.

3   Her voice is soft.

4   He likes a small dog.

5   This dress is expensive.

6   She has a big bag.

7   We saw a beautiful bird.

8   He works with friendly people.

B 다음 괄호 안에서 알맞은 것을 고르시오.

1   He has (many / much) books.

2   She didn't drink (many / much) water.

3   My brother has (much / a lot of) toys.

4   I don't have (many / much) money.

5   She has (a few / a little) friends.

6   He wants (a few / a little) sugar.

7   (Few / Little) people come to the party.

8   He knows (few / little) answers.

C 다음 우리말에 맞도록 빈칸에 알맞은 말을 **보기** 에서 골라 쓰시오.

> **보기**　hard　loudly　deeply　slowly　clearly

1 그들은 천천히 걷는다.

　→ They walk _________________.

2 그는 열심히 일한다.

　→ He works _________________.

3 우리는 크게 이야기한다.

　→ We talk _________________.

4 그녀는 명확하게 말한다.

　→ She speaks _________________.

5 그는 깊이 잠들었다.

　→ He slept _________________.

D 다음 우리말에 맞도록 빈칸에 알맞은 말을 **보기** 에서 골라 쓰시오.

> **보기**　sometimes　never　hardly　usually　always

1 그녀는 항상 제시간에 숙제를 한다.

　→ She _____________ does her homework on time.

2 나는 보통 아침 식사를 한다.

　→ I _____________ have breakfast.

3 우리는 가끔 함께 영화를 본다.

　→ We _____________ watch movies together.

4 그녀는 낯선 사람들에게 거의 이야기하지 않는다.

　→ She _____________ talks to strangers.

5 그는 절대 탄산음료를 마시지 않는다.

　→ He _____________ drinks soda.

A 다음 괄호 안에서 알맞은 것을 고르시오.

1   The bird is (color / colorful).

2   The ducks are (noise / noisy).

3   The salad is (health / healthy).

4   The flowers are (beauty / beautiful).

5   The book is (reading / readable).

6   He is very (energy / energetic).

7   She is a very (create / creative) artist.

8   The (danger / dangerous) animals are fast.

9   He is a (fame / famous) singer.

10   The (active / action) boy is riding a bike.

11   The chair is very (comfort / comfortable).

12   He is a (care / careful) student.

13   This place is very (peace / peaceful).

14   The table is (movable / movement).

15   He gave (help / helpful) tips for solving the problem.

16   This plan is very (effect / effective).

17   The results were very (impression / impressive).

18   This is a (science / scientific) tool.

19   She gave a (hope / hopeful) answer.

20   He told us a (humor / humorous) story.

B 다음 괄호 안에서 알맞은 것을 고르시오.

1   (Many / Much) students are playing basketball.

2   I have (a few / a little) pens in my pencil case.

3   She drinks (many / a lot of) water every day.

4   (Few / Little) people know this secret.

5   We need (a few / a little) candles for the cake.

6   They have (few / little) money.

7   (Many / Much) people love chocolate.

8   There is (few / little) space.

9   We need (much / a lot of) chairs for the party.

10   She didn't pour (many / much) milk to her cereal.

11   He doesn't have (many / much) time to play.

12   There are (few / little) cars on the road.

13   He has (a few / a little) hope for success.

14   We saw (few / little) tourists at the museum.

15   There is (few / little) juice in the bottle.

16   (Few / Little) shops are open in the morning.

17   We don't have (many / much) free time at school.

18   He makes (much / a lot of) mistakes in his writing.

19   (Little / Few) boats are on the river.

20   (Little / Few) rain fell during the winter.

C 다음 괄호 안에서 알맞은 것을 고르시오.

1 He walked (slow / slowly).

2 Her mood changes (easy / easily).

3 She swims (powerful / powerfully).

4 The ticket is (real / really) expensive.

5 He acted (rude / rudely).

6 They run (fast / fastly).

7 He laughed (loud / loudly).

8 We jumped (high / highly).

9 He finished the test (quick / quickly).

10 She listened to the music (careful / carefully).

11 The students studied (hard / hardly).

12 He speaks English (good / well).

13 The car moved (smooth / smoothly).

14 They entered the library (quiet / quietly).

15 (Lucky / Luckily), we can buy tickets online.

16 The teacher explained it (clear / clearly).

17 (Sad / Sadly), the museum is under construction.

18 He answered the question (correct / correctly).

19 I prepared the meal (happy / happily).

20 (Fortunate / Fortunately), we arrived just in time.

1   A: Does she exercise in the morning?

    B: Yes, she (exercises always / always exercises) before breakfast.

2   A: How often do you go to the library?

    B: I (go usually / usually go) there once a week.

3   A: Does she often watch TV before bed?

    B: No, she (rarely watches / watches rarely) TV at night.

4   A: How often do you play basketball after school?

    B: We (sometimes play / play sometimes) basketball.

5   A: Does she take the bus to school?

    B: No, she (usually walks / walks usually).

6   A: Do you use your tablet during class?

    B: No, I (never use / use never) it in class.

7   A: Are you sometimes late to class?

    B: No, (I'm never / never I'm) late.

8   A: Is she often busy after work?

    B: Yes, she (is often / often is) working on extra projects.

9   A: Is Sam always kind to his classmates?

    B: Yes, he (is always / always is) kind to everyone.

10 A: Is she never at the gym?

    B: No, she (is sometimes / sometimes is) there after work.

A 다음 우리말에 맞도록 괄호 안의 단어를 이용하여 빈칸에 알맞은 말을 쓰시오.

1 그녀는 오늘 행복하다. (happiness)

  → She is _________________ today.

2 그 해변은 아름답다. (beauty)

  → The beach is _________________.

3 그 마을은 평화롭다. (peace)

  → The village is _________________.

4 숙제는 매우 쉬웠다. (easily)

  → The homework was very _________________.

5 그는 힘찬 목소리를 가지고 있다. (power)

  → He has a _________________ voice.

6 그녀의 조언은 정말 도움이 되었다. (help)

  → Her advice was really _________________.

7 그녀에게는 그 프로젝트에 대한 창의적인 아이디어가 있었다. (create)

  → She had a _________________ idea for the project.

8 그 소파는 매우 편안하다. (comfort)

  → The sofa is very _________________.

9 그는 건강한 삶을 살려고 노력한다. (health)

  → He tries to live a _________________ life.

10 에펠 탑은 파리의 유명한 랜드마크이다. (fame)

  → The Eiffel Tower is a _________________ landmark in Paris.

11 사자는 위험한 동물이다. (danger)

  → The lion is a _________________ animal.

12 그 노인은 매우 친절하다. (friend)

  → The old man is very _________________.

 다음 우리말에 맞도록 괄호 안의 단어를 이용하여 빈칸에 알맞은 말을 쓰시오.

1 그 개가 크게 짖었다. (loud)

   → The dog barked ___________________.

2 새가 하늘 높이 날고 있다. (high)

   → The bird is flying ___________________ in the sky.

3 그녀는 빗속에서 안전하게 차를 몰았다. (safe)

   → She drove the car ___________________ in the rain.

4 그녀는 문 앞에서 나를 따뜻하게 맞이했다. (warm)

   → She greeted me ___________________ at the door.

5 그는 주말에 늦게 잠자리에 든다. (late)

   → He goes to bed ___________________ on weekends.

6 그녀는 내 가까이에 앉았다. (near)

   → She sat ___________________ me.

7 그는 최근에 도착했다. (recent)

   → He arrived ___________________.

8 그 팀은 열심히 훈련하고 있다. (hard)

   → The team is training ___________________.

9 그는 발표하는 동안 명확하게 말한다. (clear)

   → He speaks ___________________ during his presentation.

10 그녀는 수학을 정말 잘한다. (real)

   → She is ___________________ good at math.

11 별들이 밝게 빛나고 있다. (bright)

   → The stars are shining ___________________.

12 꽃들이 햇빛을 받아 자연스럽게 피었다. (natural)

   → The flowers bloomed ___________________ in the sunlight.

C 다음 문장의 밑줄 친 부분을 괄호 안의 우리말에 맞도록 어법상 바르게 고쳐 문장을 다시 쓰시오.

1 She bought <u>few</u> apples. (그녀는 사과를 몇 개 샀다.)

→ ____

2 He poured <u>little</u> water into the glass. (그는 컵에 약간의 물을 부었다.)

→ ____

3 We took <u>a little</u> photos. (우리는 몇 장의 사진을 찍었다.)

→ ____

4 <u>A few</u> people solve the problems. (거의 아무도 그 문제를 풀지 못한다.)

→ ____

5 We will stay <u>a little</u> more minutes. (우리는 몇 분 더 머무를 것이다.)

→ ____

6 She needs <u>little</u> rest after work. (그녀는 퇴근 후 약간의 휴식이 필요하다.)

→ ____

7 He has <u>a little</u> confidence. (그는 자신감이 거의 없다.)

→ ____

8 He has <u>few</u> energy after school. (그는 방과 후에 기운이 거의 없다.)

→ ____

9 She made <u>few</u> phone calls. (그녀는 몇 통의 전화를 걸었다.)

→ ____

10 He made <u>a few</u> mistakes on his test. (그는 시험에서 실수를 거의 하지 않았다.)

→ ____

11 I need <u>few</u> pens for my class. (나는 수업에서 쓸 몇 자루의 펜이 필요하다.)

→ ____

12 He knows <u>a few</u> songs. (그는 노래를 거의 모른다.)

→ ____

13 There are <u>little</u> buses running at night. (밤에 운행하는 버스가 몇 대 있다.)

→ ____

14 I have <u>a few</u> opportunities to speak English. (나는 영어를 말할 기회가 거의 없다.)

→ ____

15 We have <u>little</u> bread for sandwiches. (우리는 샌드위치를 만들 빵이 약간 있다.)

→ ____

D 다음 괄호 안의 단어들을 바르게 배열하시오.

1 (always / breakfast / we / have / .)

→ ____

2 (usually / they / the bus / take / .)

→ ____

3 (rarely / my old friends / I / see / .)

→ ____

4 (I / eat / hardly / sweets / .)

→ ____

5 (often / camping / we / go / .)

→ ____

6 (rarely / we / to the countryside / go / .)

→ ____

7 (she / wears / sometimes / bright colors / .)

→ ____

8 (drinks / usually / tea / she / .)

→ ____

9 (complain / they / about anything / rarely / .)

→ ____

10 (I / listen to / often / a podcast / .)

→ ____

11 (usually / he / for his neighbors / cookies / baked / .)

→ ____

12 (he / goes out / without his phone / never / .)

→ ____

13 (hardly / we / travel / during the winter / .)

→ ____

14 (sometimes / she / borrows / from the library / books / .)

→ ____

15 (always / my mom / my favorite dish / makes / .)

→ ____

1 다음 중 형용사와 부사가 <u>잘못</u> 짝지어진 것은?

① soft – softly
② slow – slowly
③ happy – happily
④ love – lovely
⑤ good – well

[2–4] 다음 중 빈칸에 들어갈 말로 가장 적절한 것을 고르시오.

2

He is a _______ person.

① too
② very
③ friendly
④ politely
⑤ kindly

3

They crossed the street _______.

① care
② careful
③ caring
④ carefully
⑤ careless

4

_______ students arrived early for the class.

① Much
② Little
③ A little
④ A few
⑤ Any

[5–6] 다음 우리말에 맞도록 빈칸에 들어갈 말로 가장 적절한 것을 고르시오.

5

• 내 지갑에 돈이 거의 없다.
→ I have _______ money in my wallet.

① little
② a little
③ a few
④ few
⑤ much

6

• 그녀는 패스트푸드를 거의 먹지 않는다.
→ She _______ eats fast food.

① never
② rarely
③ usually
④ sometimes
⑤ always

7 다음 대화의 빈칸에 공통으로 들어갈 말로 가장 적절한 것은?

A: How can I get a ______ score on the basketball test?
B: You need to jump ______.

① good
② nice
③ perfect
④ poor
⑤ high

[8-10] 다음 우리말에 맞도록 빈칸에 알맞은 말을 쓰시오.

8

그는 나에게 숙제에 관한 질문을 몇 개 했다.

→ He asked me ________ ______________ questions about the homework.

9

그녀는 매운 음식을 절대 먹지 않는다.

→ She ______________ eats spicy food.

10

나는 내 남동생을 좋아하고, 내 남동생도 나를 좋아한다.

→ I like my brother, and my brother likes me ______________.

11 다음 중 usually가 들어갈 위치로 알맞은 것은?

She ① wears ② a hat ③ in ④ summer ⑤.

①   ②   ③   ④   ⑤

12 다음 글의 밑줄 친 부분 중 어법상 <u>틀린</u> 곳은?

It was a ①<u>happy</u> day for Sam. He woke up ②<u>early</u> and smiled brightly. The sun shone ③<u>warm</u> and made him feel good. Sam ate a delicious breakfast ④<u>quickly</u>. Then, he ran excitedly to meet his friends. They played ⑤<u>happily</u> all day.

①   ②   ③   ④   ⑤

[13-15] 다음 문장에서 어법상 <u>틀린</u> 곳을 찾아 바르게 고치시오.

13

I always exercise regular in the morning.

______________ → ______________

14

Honest, I don't know the answer.

______________ → ______________

15

How many water do you drink every day?

______________ → ______________

[16-17] 다음 중 빈칸에 들어갈 말로 적절하지 <u>않은</u> 것을 고르시오.

16

__________ students understood the difficult question.

① Few   ② Many

③ A lot of   ④ A few

⑤ A little

17

There is __________ hope of success.

① lots of   ② a lot of

③ little   ④ a little

⑤ a few

18 다음 우리말에 맞도록 괄호 안의 단어를 이용하여 빈칸에 알맞은 말을 쓰시오.

그들은 경기 중에 크게 소리쳤다. (loud)

→ They shouted ______________
　 during the game.

19

다음 중 밑줄 친 부분이 어법상 틀린 것은?

① He studied English <u>hard</u>.

② She went to school <u>early</u>.

③ I <u>really</u> didn't know about it.

④ This car is <u>too</u> expensive.

⑤ <u>Sudden</u>, he changed his mind.

20

다음 두 대화의 빈칸에 공통으로 들어갈 말로 가장 적절한 것은?

- **A:** Is this bike __________?
  B: Yes, it is.
- **A:** Did he drive slowly?
  B: No, he drove __________.

① fast   ② slow

③ quick   ④ speedy

⑤ strong

[21–22] 다음 우리말에 맞도록 괄호 안의 단어들을 바르게 배열하시오.

21

그녀는 학교에 절대 늦지 않는다.
(she / never / for school / is / late / .)

→ ________________________________

22

그들은 시험공부를 거의 하지 않는다.
(hardly / they / for their exams / study / .)

→ ________________________________

23

다음 글의 밑줄 친 부분 중 어법상 옳은 것끼리 바르게 짝지어진 것은?

My sister wakes up early in the morning. She ⓐ<u>always</u> makes her bed before leaving her room. After breakfast, she often reads a book or studies ⓑ<u>quietly</u>. She sometimes goes for a walk in the park if the weather is ⓒ<u>nicely</u>. In the evening, she ⓓ<u>rare</u> watches TV because she prefers reading. Before going to bed, she ⓔ<u>usually</u> drinks a cup of tea.

① ⓐ, ⓑ

② ⓑ, ⓒ

③ ⓑ, ⓓ

④ ⓐ, ⓑ, ⓔ

⑤ ⓑ, ⓓ, ⓔ

전치사

- 전치사의 쓰임
- 장소 / 위치 전치사
- 시간 전치사와 방향 전치사
- 3형식 동사와 쓰이는 전치사

전치사의 쓰임

전치사: 명사나 대명사 앞에서 시간, 위치, 장소, 방향 등을 나타냄		
of	~의	It is a picture of my family.
about	~에 대해	Don't worry about it.
with	~와 함께	I had lunch with my friends.
for	~을 위해	Can you do this for me?
to	~에게, ~으로	It's important to me.
from	~으로부터	I got a call from your teacher.

A 다음 문장에서 전치사를 찾아 밑줄 치시오.

1 This gift is for you.

2 The cat ran to the door.

3 I played soccer with my friends.

장소 / 위치 전치사

in	~안에(사물의 내부), ~(지역)에	in the box, in Seoul
at	~(지점)에	at home, at school
on	~위에(표면에 접촉된 상태)	on the table
near	~근처에, ~가까이에	near my house
between	~사이에	between the bank and the shop
above	~보다 위에	above the mountain
under	~의 아래에, ~의 바로 밑에	under the tree
behind	~뒤에	behind the building
in front of	~앞에	in front of the door

B 다음 괄호 안에서 알맞은 것을 고르시오.

1 I live (in / at) Seoul.

2 The vase is (on / in) the table.

3 We sat (under / between) the tree.

시간 전치사와 방향 전치사		
in	~에(연도, 월, 계절, 오전, 오후)	in 2025, in March, in spring
on	~에(요일, 날짜, 특정한 날)	on Sunday, on my birthday
at	~에(시각, 시점)	at noon, at night, at 7 o'clock
before	~전에	before dinner
after	~후에	after lunch
for	~동안(기간 숫자 표현)	for 20 years
during	~동안(특정 기간 명사)	during the vacation
from	~에서부터	The train came from Seoul.
for	~을 향하여	They left for the airport.
to	~에, ~으로	She walked to the store.
toward	~을 향하여	The dog was running toward me.
up	~의 위로	He ran up the hill.
down	~의 아래로	He climbed down the ladder.

C 다음 괄호 안에서 알맞은 것을 고르시오.

1 My brother was born (in / on) 2024.

2 The wind is blowing (from / with) the east.

3 He will leave (for / under) Canada.

3형식 동사와 쓰이는 전치사	
쓰임	뜻
replace A with B	A를 B로 대체하다
mix A with B	A와 B를 섞다
provide A with B	A에게 B를 제공하다
thank A for B	A에게 B에 대해 감사하다
compensate A for B	A에게 B에 대해 보상하다
mistake A for B	A를 B로 착각하다
blame A for B	A를 B에 대해 비난하다
criticize A for B	A를 B에 대해 비판하다
inform A of B	A에게 B를 알리다
rob(deprive) A of B	A에게서 B를 빼앗다
prevent(stop, keep) A from B	A가 B하는 것을 막다
prohibit A from B	A가 B하는 것을 금지하다

D 다음 괄호 안에서 알맞은 것을 고르시오.

1 I will replace the old phone (of / with) a new one.

2 He mixed rice (of / with) beans.

3 She stopped him (to / from) eating too much.

A 다음 문장에서 전치사를 찾아 밑줄 치시오.

1   He is in the room.

2   The book is on the desk.

3   We met at the bus stop.

4   The cat is under the chair.

5   The tree is between two houses.

6   The store closes at 7 p.m.

7   She talks about her family.

8   He eats lunch with his mom.

B 다음 괄호 안에서 알맞은 것을 고르시오.

1   He lives (in / at) a big city.

2   She works (at / of) a hospital.

3   There is a pencil (on / to) the floor.

4   The cat is (in / of) the box.

5   We walk (near / with) my house.

6   The river flows (above / between) the mountains.

7   The airplane is flying (above / about) the clouds.

8   He parked the car (with / behind) the building.

C 다음 우리말에 맞도록 빈칸에 알맞은 말을 보기 에서 골라 쓰시오.

보기 in on at

1 내 생일은 4월에 있다.

→ My birthday is _______________ April.

2 그는 월요일에 시험이 있다.

→ He has a test _______________ Monday.

3 우리는 정오에 점심을 먹는다.

→ We have lunch _______________ noon.

4 나는 첫 등교일에 긴장했다.

→ I was nervous _______________ my first day of school.

5 그들은 3시에 회의를 할 것이다.

→ They will have a meeting _______________ 3 o'clock.

D 다음 우리말에 맞도록 빈칸에 알맞은 말을 보기 에서 골라 쓰시오.

보기 with for of from

1 그는 낡은 의자를 새 것으로 교체했다.

→ He replaced the old chair ____________ a new one.

2 그는 수업에 대해 선생님께 감사했다.

→ He thanked his teacher ____________ the lesson.

3 그들은 나에게 시험 결과를 알려 주었다.

→ They informed me ____________ the exam results.

4 그 의사는 환자가 흡연하는 것을 막았다.

→ The doctor prevented the patient ____________ smoking.

5 회사는 근로자의 노고에 대해 보상해 주었다.

→ The company compensated the worker ____________ his hard work.

A 다음 괄호 안에서 알맞은 것을 고르시오.

1   We saw a map (of / to) the world.

2   The book is (to / for) children.

3   She learned (for / about) space in science class.

4   The sign is (of / for) safety.

5   He heard the sound (to / of) the rain.

6   I sent a letter (to / in) my sister.

7   I love the smell (of / to) coffee.

8   He worried (with / about) the test.

9   They showed the picture (to / for) the class.

10   We read a book (about / from) animals.

11   They apologized (in / to) their neighbors.

12   He knows the name (of / to) that place.

13   They introduced me (to / from) their family.

14   She is cooking (of / with) her mother.

15   The color (of / from) the sky is blue.

16   He opened the lid (of / to) the box.

17   I need to think (about / with) my future.

18   She is playing (of / with) her dog.

19   He received a call (to / from) his mother.

20   The cake is (of / for) the birthday party.

 다음 괄호 안에서 알맞은 것을 고르시오.

1   I live (in / on) Korea.

2   We study (of / at) school.

3   He sleeps (in / of) the bedroom.

4   There is a picture (in / on) the wall.

5   We got (on / above) the airplane.

6   She is (under / in) the bathroom.

7   The clock is (in / above) the door.

8   We stayed (at / for) home all day.

9   She is (in / above) the library.

10   She hid (behind / in front of) the curtain.

11   She spoke (under / in front of) her classmates.

12   She found her keys (of / under) the sofa.

13   We arrived (at / to) the airport.

14   The students followed (above / behind) the teacher.

15   He walked (on / under) the sidewalk.

16   I sat (on / above) the chair.

17   We camped (under / above) the stars.

18   We shopped (at / between) the mall.

19   We waited (in front of / behind of) the store.

20   There is a bridge (on / between) the two cities.

C 다음 괄호 안에서 알맞은 것을 고르시오.

1   The class starts (at / in) 9 a.m.

2   He goes to bed (at / on) midnight.

3   She moved to New York (at / in) 2020.

4   She ran (of / toward) the bus.

5   John exercises (in / on) the morning.

6   The cat climbed (up / from) the tree.

7   She swims a lot (in / on) summer.

8   He walked (up / of) the stairs.

9   They ate snacks (for / during) the break.

10   Jane got married (on / in) May 25th.

11   They are heading (on / for) the airport.

12   They stayed silent (for / during) the meeting.

13   Mike visited her family (on / in) Thanksgiving Day.

14   We are going to stay here (at / for) five days.

15   They traveled to Europe (in / at) winter.

16   He took a train (for / during) Busan.

17   Eric usually wakes up late (on / in) Saturday.

18   The dog jumped (of / toward) me.

19   We will be on vacation (for / during) two weeks.

20   We met for the first time (in / on) November.

D 다음 대화의 괄호 안에서 알맞은 것을 고르시오.

1 A: My phone is too old. It doesn't work well anymore.

   B: You should replace it (to / with) a new model.

2 A: How did you get that purple color?

   B: I mixed red (with / from) blue.

3 A: Here's the map you asked for.

   B: Thank you (for / from) your help!

4 A: Why are you drinking juice with your coffee?

   B: I mistook the orange juice (of / for) milk.

5 A: Why are the plants not growing well?

   B: The tall buildings deprive them (of / from) sunlight.

6 A: Did she inform you (of / about) the deadline?

   B: No, I had no idea! When is it due?

7 A: Why can't we talk loudly in the library?

   B: Because the library prohibits visitors (to / from) making loud noises.

8 A: Do you offer Wi-Fi at the hotel?

   B: Yes, we provide all guests (with / of) free Wi-Fi.

9 A: Why is the teacher so strict today?

   B: She wants to prevent students (with / from) talking during class.

10 A: I forgot to bring your coffee this morning.

   B: You can compensate me (for / with) that with another one.

A 다음 우리말에 맞도록 빈칸에 알맞은 말을 쓰시오.

1 Tom은 그의 휴대폰을 테이블 위에 놓았다.

→ Tom put his phone _______________ the table.

2 그녀는 달빛 아래에서 걸었다.

→ She walked _______________ the moonlight.

3 우리는 과거에 대해 많이 생각하지 않는다.

→ We don't think much _______________ the past.

4 그녀는 입구 근처에 서 있었다.

→ She stood _______________ the entrance.

5 그녀는 신발을 문 뒤에 놓았다.

→ She placed her shoes _______________ the door.

6 그는 지금 집 앞에 있지 않다.

→ He is not _______________ the house right now.

7 그 고양이는 더 이상 상자 안에 있지 않다.

→ The cat is not _______________ the box anymore.

8 그녀는 그녀의 직업에 대해 불평하지 않는다.

→ She doesn't complain _______________ her job.

9 거울이 세면대 위에 있다.

→ The mirror is _______________ the sink.

10 그녀는 작은 마을 출신이다.

→ She comes _______________ a small town.

11 그녀는 휴대폰을 책상 아래로 떨어뜨렸다.

→ She dropped her phone _______________ the desk.

12 파나마는 북아메리카와 남아메리카 사이에 있다.

→ Panama is _______________ North America and South America.

B 다음 우리말에 맞도록 빈칸에 알맞은 말을 쓰시오.

1   아버지는 1990년에 대학교를 졸업했다.

→ My father graduated from university ______________ 1990.

2   Sam은 8시에 집을 떠났다.

→ Sam left home ______________ 8 o'clock.

3   나는 일요일에 새 프로젝트를 시작할 것이다.

→ I will start the new project ______________ Sunday.

4   그녀는 운동 전에 항상 스트레칭을 한다.

→ She always stretches ______________ exercise.

5   그는 점심을 먹은 후 낮잠을 잤다.

→ He took a nap ______________ lunch.

6   그는 밸런타인데이에 나에게 전화했다.

→ He called me ______________ Valentine's Day.

7   우리는 30분 동안 버스를 기다렸다.

→ We waited for the bus ______________ 30 minutes.

8   그는 지붕을 고치기 위해 사다리를 올라갔다.

→ He climbed ______________ the ladder to fix the roof.

9   그들은 휴가 동안 콘서트를 즐겼다.

→ They enjoyed the concert ______________ their vacation.

10   빛은 태양에서 지구로 이동한다.

→ Light travels ______________ the Sun to the Earth.

11   우리는 저녁에 함께 식사를 한다.

→ We have dinner together ______________ the evening.

12   우리는 한 시간 동안 전화 통화를 했다.

→ We talked on the phone ______________ an hour.

C 다음 우리말에 맞도록 괄호 안의 단어들과 전치사를 이용하여 문장을 완성하시오.

1 그녀는 벤치에 앉았다. (the bench)

→ She sat _______________________________.

2 학생들은 나무 아래에 모였다. (the tree)

→ The students gathered _______________________________.

3 내 생일은 3월 24일이다. (March 24th)

→ My birthday is _______________________________.

4 인터넷은 1990년대에 널리 사용되었다. (the 1990s)

→ The internet became widely used _______________________________.

5 그들은 2시간 동안 농구를 했다. (two hours)

→ They played basketball _______________________________.

6 그 집의 지붕은 빨간색이다. (the house)

→ The roof _______________________________ is red.

7 그들은 서로 다른 나라에서 왔다. (different countries)

→ They came _______________________________.

8 지하철역이 내 집 근처에 있다. (my house)

→ The subway station is _______________________________.

9 그는 그의 친구들과 함께 쇼핑몰에 갔다. (his friends)

→ He went to the mall _______________________________.

10 내 아파트 뒤에 작은 정원이 있다. (my apartment)

→ There is a small garden _______________________________.

11 우리는 쇼핑몰 앞에서 만났다. (the shopping mall)

→ We met _______________________________.

12 많은 학생들이 방학 동안 휴식을 취한다. (the vacation)

→ Many students take a break _______________________________.

13 우리는 보통 점심 식사 후에 산책을 한다. (lunch)

→ We usually take a walk _______________________________.

14 그 가게는 자정 전에 문을 닫는다. (midnight)

→ The store closes _______________________________.

15 기차는 정오에 도착할 것이다. (noon)

→ The train will arrive _______________________________.

 다음 문장의 밑줄 친 부분을 알맞은 전치사로 고쳐 문장을 다시 쓰시오.

1   I replace the batteries <u>of</u> new ones.

    → ____

2   If you mix blue <u>for</u> yellow, you get green.

    → ____

3   They provided us <u>to</u> useful information.

    → ____

4   He thanked her <u>on</u> her kindness.

    → ____

5   She informed me <u>from</u> the meeting time.

    → ____

6   I stopped him <u>to</u> making a big mistake.

    → ____

7   He mistook me <u>with</u> my older brother.

    → ____

8   The mask keeps me <u>to</u> breathing in dust.

    → ____

9   She criticized her friend <u>of</u> being late.

    → ____

10   They robbed the bank <u>to</u> five million dollars.

    → ____

11   The fans blamed the coach <u>of</u> the team's loss.

    → ____

12   The storm deprived the village <u>from</u> electricity.

    → ____

13   The teacher prohibited us <u>to</u> talking during the test.

    → ____

14   I prevent my dog <u>to</u> running into the street.

    → ____

15   The store compensated me <u>with</u> the damaged product.

    → ____

[1–3] 다음 중 빈칸에 들어갈 말로 가장 적절한 것을 고르시오.

1

We live _______ China.

① on   ② with

③ at   ④ in

⑤ above

2

He participated in the Olympics _______ 2020.

① in   ② on

③ at   ④ of

⑤ for

3

He waited _______ two hours.

① of   ② during

③ for   ④ from

⑤ with

4 다음 중 밑줄 친 부분의 쓰임이 <u>어색한</u> 것은?

① He was born <u>in</u> 2011.

② She had dinner <u>with</u> him.

③ I wake up early <u>in</u> Thursdays.

④ The books are <u>on</u> the shelf.

⑤ The school is <u>near</u> my house.

[5–6] 다음 중 빈칸에 들어갈 말로 적절하지 <u>않은</u> 것을 고르시오.

5

They stand _______ the door.

① at   ② near

③ above   ④ behind

⑤ in front of

6

The key is _______ the sofa.

① on   ② to

③ near   ④ under

⑤ behind

[7-8] 다음 중 밑줄 친 부분의 쓰임이 어색한 것을 고르시오.

7

① She smiled <u>at</u> me.

② I work hard <u>of</u> my future.

③ He knows a lot <u>about</u> history.

④ He is traveling <u>with</u> his family.

⑤ They are <u>from</u> the United States.

8

① It often snows <u>in</u> winter.

② The movie starts <u>on</u> 10 p.m.

③ The sun rises <u>in</u> the morning.

④ We exchange gifts <u>on</u> Christmas Day.

⑤ The online event will be live <u>at</u> noon.

[9-11] 다음 우리말에 맞도록 빈칸에 들어갈 말로 가장 적절한 것을 고르시오.

9

- 내 집은 기차역과 대학교 사이에 있다.
→ My house is __________ the train station and the university.

① of   ② on

③ during   ④ between

⑤ in front of

10

- 그들은 출구를 향해 달려갔다.
→ They ran __________ the exit.

① in   ② on

③ at   ④ behind

⑤ toward

11

- 그 학교는 학생들에게 건강한 점심을 제공한다.
→ The school provides students __________ healthy lunches.

① to   ② of

③ of   ④ with

⑤ from

12 다음 글의 밑줄 친 부분 중 쓰임이 어색한 것은?

Jenny walked ①<u>to</u> the kitchen and made tea. She sat ②<u>on</u> the sofa and read a book. Her cat jumped ③<u>with</u> joy onto her lap. She placed the book ④<u>above</u> the table and stood up. Then, she went outside ⑤<u>for</u> a walk.

①   ②   ③   ④   ⑤

[13–14] 다음 대화의 빈칸에 공통으로 들어갈 말로 가장 적절한 것을 고르시오.

13

A: The company will compensate you ______ the delay.
B: Thank you ______ your help.

① on   ② of
③ about   ④ in
⑤ for

14

A: Do you want to meet ______ the café later?
B: Sure! Let's meet ______ noon.

① on   ② in
③ at   ④ of
⑤ with

[15–17] 다음 우리말에 맞도록 빈칸에 들어갈 알맞은 말을 쓰시오.

15

그들은 전화로 세 시간 동안 이야기했다.

→ They talked on the phone ______________ three hours.

16

의사는 환자가 정크 푸드 먹는 것을 금지했다.

→ The doctor prohibited the patient ______________ eating junk food.

17

선생님은 학생들에게 시험 날짜를 알려 주었다.

→ The teacher informed the students ______________ the exam date.

18 다음 대화의 빈칸에 들어갈 말이 바르게 짝지어진 것은?

A: Why are you upset with Tom?
B: He blamed me ______ the small mistake in our report.
A: Take it easy. He was just trying to keep you ______ making a bigger error.

① on - from
② for - from
③ from - to
④ from - for
⑤ for - to

19

They took a photo in front at the museum.

__________ → __________

20

The thief robbed the man on his wallet.

__________ → __________

21

The heavy rain kept us to going outside.

__________ → __________

22 다음 두 대화의 빈칸에 들어갈 말이 바르게 짝지어진 것은?

- A: How long did she practice the piano?
  B: She practiced piano ______ 20 days.
- A: When did you go on a trip?
  B: I traveled ______ my vacation.

① in - on
② during - for
③ for - during
④ for - in
⑤ during - during

23 다음 글의 밑줄 친 부분 중 쓰임이 적절한 것끼리 바르게 짝지어진 것은?

Emma wanted to replace her old phone ⓐ<u>with</u> a new one. Her friend informed her ⓑ<u>at</u> a great discount at the store. She thanked him ⓒ<u>for</u> his help. At the store, she almost mistook a customer ⓓ<u>with</u> a staff member. She bought the new phone and felt satisfied.

① ⓐ, ⓑ
② ⓐ, ⓒ
③ ⓑ, ⓒ
④ ⓐ, ⓒ, ⓓ
⑤ ⓑ, ⓒ, ⓓ

5

현재완료

현재완료의 개념과 형태

개념	과거에 일어난 일이 현재까지 영향을 미칠 때 사용 '완료, 경험, 계속, 결과'의 의미를 가짐		
형태 (긍정문)	주어 + have / has + 과거분사		
	I / You / We / They → have + 과거분사 He / She / It → has + 과거분사		She has worked here. I have eaten sushi before.
	과거분사	규칙 동사(-ed): worked, played 등	
		불규칙 동사: gone, eaten 등	

* 동사 변화의 과거분사형 활용: 1. 완료형, 2. 수동태
* 현재완료는 과거의 특정 시점을 나타내는 말(ago, yesterday, after 등)과 함께 쓰지 않는다.

A 다음 괄호 안의 형태에 맞도록 go를 이용하여 빈칸에 알맞은 말을 쓰시오.

1 He ____________ to bed. (과거형)

2 He _________ ____________ to bed. (현재완료형)

현재완료의 부정문과 의문문

부정문	주어 + <u>have / has + not</u> + 과거분사 (haven't / hasn't)	
	I / You / We / They → haven't	I haven't seen that movie.
	He / She / It → hasn't	He hasn't finished his work.
의문문	Have / Has + 주어 + 과거분사 ~?	
	I / You / We / They → Have	Have you traveled abroad? - Yes, I have. / No, I haven't.
	He / She / It → Has	Has he eaten lunch? - Yes, he has. / No, he hasn't.

B 다음 중 옳은 문장에 동그라미 하시오.

1 I don't have done it. （　）

I haven't done it. （　）

2 Has he finished it? （　）

Does he have finished it? （　）

용법	설명	주요 부사	예문
완료	과거에 시작된 일이 막 완료됨 '(방금, 이미, 아직) ~했다'	just already yet	I have just completed the project. Have you already done your homework?
경험	현재까지의 경험 '~한 적이 있다(없다)'	never ever before	I have never been to Japan. Have you ever seen that movie?

C 다음 문장을 우리말로 해석하시오.

1 She has already started the work.

→ ______________________________________

2 He has visited Paris several times.

→ ______________________________________

용법	설명	주요 부사	예문
계속	과거에 시작되어 현재까지 지속되는 상황 '계속 ~해 왔다'	for, since	They have been friends for 10 years. She has worked at this company since 2010.
결과	과거의 행동이 현재까지 영향을 미침 주로 현재 상태를 강조 '(그 결과 지금) ~한 상태이다'		He has broken his leg.

D 다음 문장을 우리말로 해석하시오.

1 I have lived here for five years.

→ ______________________________________

2 I have lost my keys.

→ ______________________________________

A 다음 문장에서 현재완료형에 밑줄 치시오.

1 I have joined a contest.

2 We have done the work.

3 He has played basketball.

4 I haven't seen that movie.

5 He has returned my book.

6 I have answered all the questions.

7 We have visited a historical place.

8 She has studied English since last year.

B 다음 괄호 안에서 알맞은 것을 고르시오.

1 (Did / Have) you ever played chess?

2 (Has / Have) he ever been to Jeju?

3 I have never (try / tried) that dish.

4 I (haven't / don't have) visited a zoo.

5 They have (been / being) to the beach.

6 We have (stayed / staying) in this house.

7 I have never (met / meet) a famous person.

8 We (has / have) not celebrated Christmas together.

 다음 우리말에 맞도록 괄호 안의 단어를 이용하여 현재완료형 문장을 완성하시오.

1 나는 이미 이 책을 읽었다. (read)

   → I ___________ already ___________ this book.

2 그녀는 벌써 저녁을 먹었다. (eat)

   → She ___________ already ___________ dinner.

3 그들은 파티에 막 도착했다. (arrive)

   → They ___________ just ___________ at the party.

4 그는 파리에 가 본 적이 있다. (be)

   → He ___________ ___________ to Paris.

5 나는 전에 그를 본 적이 있다. (see)

   → I ___________ ___________ him before.

6 그들은 그 장소에 대해 들어 본 적이 있다. (hear)

   → They ___________ ___________ of that place.

D **다음 우리말에 맞도록 괄호 안의 단어들을 이용하여 현재완료형 문장을 완성하시오.**

1 우리는 그녀를 만난 적이 결코 없다. (never, meet)

   → We ___________ ___________ ___________ her.

2 나는 대중 앞에서 노래를 부른 적이 결코 없다. (never, sing)

   → I ___________ ___________ ___________ in public.

3 그는 비행기를 타 본 적이 한 번도 없다. (never, fly)

   → He ___________ ___________ ___________ on an airplane.

4 너는 전에 그것을 해 본 적이 있니? (do)

   → ___________ you ___________ that before?

5 너는 한국 음식을 요리해 본 적이 있니? (cook)

   → ___________ you ever ___________ Korean food?

6 그녀는 전에 번지 점프를 시도해 본 적이 있니? (try)

   → ___________ she ___________ bungee jumping before?

A 다음 중 현재완료형 문장에는 ○, 그 외의 문장에는 X를 표시하시오.

1 I have played tennis. ( )

2 She went to France. ( )

3 He has visited the park. ( )

4 He told me a good story. ( )

5 I haven't seen the play. ( )

6 They have played chess. ( )

7 He met many friends there. ( )

8 They have stayed at a hotel. ( )

9 She has never seen snow. ( )

10 I have bought a new book. ( )

11 We have a wonderful idea. ( )

12 They have gone to the beach. ( )

13 I haven't visited the zoo yet. ( )

14 She read that book two years ago. ( )

15 We wanted to watch that movie. ( )

16 She is washing the dishes now. ( )

17 I did not do my homework yesterday. ( )

18 We have not discussed the project. ( )

19 We have traveled to many countries. ( )

20 She finished her artwork yesterday. ( )

1   We have never climbed a mountain together.   (경험, 계속)

2   He has just left the office.   (완료, 경험)

3   I have traveled abroad for work twice.   (완료, 경험)

4   I have already finished the mission.   (계속, 완료)

5   They have never seen a play in the theater.   (경험, 계속)

6   We have just received the news.   (완료, 결과)

7   I have lived in this country for seven years.   (계속, 완료)

8   I have just spoken to her.   (결과, 완료)

9   She has worked in the school for a long time.   (계속, 완료)

10   They have just finished their work.   (완료, 경험)

11   We have seen that film before.   (경험, 완료)

12   We have known each other since childhood.   (경험, 계속)

13   She has tried swimming before.   (완료, 경험)

14   We have just ended the meeting.   (완료, 계속)

15   They have studied Korean history for two years.   (계속, 결과)

16   I have already answered the question.   (계속, 완료)

17   They have listened to this song together before.   (경험, 계속)

18   I have completely forgotten my homework.   (결과, 경험)

19   I have been awake for twenty hours.   (계속, 완료)

20   She has broken her arm.   (경험, 결과)

C 다음 문장을 괄호 안의 지시에 따라 바꿔 쓰시오.

1 He plays the piano. (현재완료형으로)

→ ____

2 I bought a new jacket. (현재완료형으로)

→ ____

3 We ran in a race. (현재완료형으로)

→ ____

4 I have packed my bag. (부정문으로)

→ ____

5 We have decided to go. (부정문으로)

→ ____

6 She has closed the door. (부정문으로)

→ ____

7 We have stayed in a hotel. (never 추가)

→ ____

8 She has been to a concert. (never 추가)

→ ____

9 They have seen a tiger. (never 추가)

→ ____

10 She has gone camping. (의문문으로)

→ ____

11 You have been to the mountains. (의문문으로)

→ ____

12 You have ever written a poem. (의문문으로)

→ ____

13 He has ever tried skydiving. (의문문으로)

→ ____

14 You have ever lived in another country. (의문문으로)

→ ____

15 You have ever been to a music festival. (의문문으로)

→ ____

 다음 대화의 괄호 안에서 알맞은 것을 고르시오.

1 A: Has he (read / reads) this book?

   B: No, he (hasn't / doesn't).

2 A: (Has / Have) she painted a picture?

   B: Yes, she (does / has).

3 A: (Has / Did) he sing in a choir last year?

   B: No, he (hasn't / didn't).

4 A: Have you ever (ran / run) in a marathon?

   B: Yes, I (has / have).

5 A: (Do / Have) they celebrate Christmas every year?

   B: No, they (don't / haven't).

6 A: (Has / Have) your son ever ridden a horse?

   B: No, he (hasn't / haven't).

7 A: Has she ever (spoke / spoken) to a famous actor?

   B: No, she (has / hasn't).

8 A: Have you visited the museum (ago / before)?

   B: No, I (have / haven't).

9 A: Have you (were / been) to a K-pop concert?

   B: Yes, I (been / have).

10 A: Has he (changes / changed) his clothes?

   B: No, he (haven't / hasn't).

A 다음 우리말에 맞도록 빈칸에 알맞은 말을 쓰시오.

1 나는 이틀 동안 계속 아팠다.
→ I _______________ _______________ sick for two days.

2 그들은 지금 막 결정을 내렸다.
→ They _______________ just _______________ a decision.

3 그는 이미 티켓을 구매했다.
→ He _______________ _______________ bought the tickets.

4 나는 그런 영화를 본 적이 있다.
→ I _______________ _______________ a movie like that.

5 그는 5년 동안 영어를 공부해 왔다.
→ He has _______________ English _______________ five years.

6 그녀는 2023년부터 이 마을에 살았다.
→ She _______________ lived in this town _______________ 2023.

7 그들은 9시부터 여기에 쭉 있었다.
→ They _______________ _______________ here since 9 o'clock.

8 나는 이제 막 이 어려운 기사를 다 읽었다.
→ I _______________ just _______________ this difficult article.

9 그 남자는 그녀에게 많은 편지를 써 왔다.
→ The man _______________ _______________ many letters to her.

10 그는 점심시간부터 그림을 그렸다.
→ He _______________ _______________ a picture since lunchtime.

11 그들은 역사적인 장소에 방문해 본 적이 있다.
→ They _______________ _______________ a historical place.

12 그녀의 아이들은 어젯밤부터 컴퓨터 게임을 하고 있다.
→ Her children _______________ _______________ computer games since last night.

 다음 우리말에 맞도록 빈칸에 알맞은 말을 쓰시오.

1 나는 책상을 청소하지 않았다.

→ I have ___________ ___________ the desk.

2 나는 전에 눈을 본 적이 결코 없다.

→ I ___________ ___________ seen snow before.

3 우리는 아직 그 주제를 논의하지 않았다.

→ We ___________ ___________ the topic yet.

4 나는 아직 그 문제를 해결하지 못했다.

→ I ___________ ___________ that problem yet.

5 그는 초콜릿 케이크를 먹어 본 적이 결코 없다.

→ He has ___________ ___________ chocolate cake.

6 그들은 아직 축구 경기를 시작하지 않았다.

→ They ___________ ___________ the soccer match yet.

7 그가 그녀에게 방금 전화했나요?

→ ___________ he just ___________ her?

8 그는 이미 생각을 바꾸었나요?

→ Has he ___________ ___________ his mind?

9 당신은 매운 음식을 먹어 본 적이 있나요?

→ Have you ___________ ___________ spicy food?

10 그녀는 이미 그녀의 사무실을 떠났나요?

→ ___________ she already ___________ her office?

11 그들은 해외여행을 해 본 적이 있나요?

→ ___________ they ___________ traveled abroad?

12 그녀는 그 메시지에 이미 답변을 했나요?

→ ___________ she ___________ replied to that message?

C 다음 중 어법상 옳은 문장에는 ○, 틀린 문장에는 X를 표시한 후, 틀린 곳을 바르게 고치시오.

1   I have traveled by train.   (   )

_______________ → _______________

2   Has he broke the glass?   (   )

_______________ → _______________

3   They has played the piano.   (   )

_______________ → _______________

4   He has saw a tiger at the zoo.   (   )

_______________ → _______________

5   Have you fixed my computer?   (   )

_______________ → _______________

6   Have they plan the event already?   (   )

_______________ → _______________

7   We have eaten at that restaurant.   (   )

_______________ → _______________

8   We have took a walk in the park.   (   )

_______________ → _______________

9   Have he told her the truth?   (   )

_______________ → _______________

10 We have never taken a long trip.   (   )

_______________ → _______________

11 I don't have written a song yet.   (   )

_______________ → _______________

12 They have never experience a cooking class. (   )

_______________ → _______________

13 I have never swum in the ocean.   (   )

_______________ → _______________

14 They have never been to a theme park.   (   )

_______________ → _______________

15 He has worked in the garden ago.   (   )

_______________ → _______________

 다음 괄호 안의 단어들을 바르게 배열하시오.

1 (I / the window / opened / have /.)

→ _______________________________________

2 (has / Amy / cooked / dinner /.)

→ _______________________________________

3 (has / he / packed / his bag /.)

→ _______________________________________

4 (done / my son / has / his chores /.)

→ _______________________________________

5 (they / at the park / arrived / have /.)

→ _______________________________________

6 (has / she / moved / to a new house /.)

→ _______________________________________

7 (practiced / have / we / English / for 3 years /.)

→ _______________________________________

8 (I / had / have / never / a pet /.)

→ _______________________________________

9 (have / never / we / gone on a picnic /.)

→ _______________________________________

10 (not / she / tasted / has / the new cookies /.)

→ _______________________________________

11 (they / paid / have / the bill / ?)

→ _______________________________________

12 (he / has / learned / the skills / ?)

→ _______________________________________

13 (to the gym / she / gone / has / ?)

→ _______________________________________

14 (you / heard of / have / that singer / ?)

→ _______________________________________

15 (built / your sons / have / a sandcastle / ?)

→ _______________________________________

1 다음 중 현재완료형 문장은?

① I am eating lunch now.

② I have just eaten lunch.

③ I will eat lunch later.

④ I eat lunch every day.

⑤ I ate lunch yesterday.

4

I __________ him a long time ago.

① met   ② meet

③ meets   ④ have met

⑤ will meet

2 다음 중 밑줄 친 부분을 어법상 바르게 고친 것은?

He <u>stay</u> at home since last Friday.

① stays   ② stayed

③ will stay   ④ is staying

⑤ has stayed

5

Have you __________ to the Alps?

① were   ② are

③ been   ④ went

⑤ being

[3-5] 다음 중 빈칸에 들어갈 말로 가장 적절한 것을 고르시오.

3

They have already __________ home.

① go   ② went

③ gone   ④ goes

⑤ going

[6-7] 다음 우리말에 맞도록 빈칸에 알맞은 말을 쓰시오.

6

나는 전에 기린을 본 적이 있다.

→ I __________ __________ a giraffe before.

그녀는 기타를 연주해 본 적이 없다.

→ She has __________ __________ the guitar.

 [8-9] 다음 중 어법상 틀린 것을 고르시오.

8

① I have visited London twice.

② He has already eaten lunch.

③ We have seen that movie before.

④ They have gone to the store yesterday.

⑤ They have lived here for seven years.

9

① I have just seen him.

② He has never been to Japan.

③ She has finished her speech.

④ She has just send the email.

⑤ He has learned math for two years.

10 다음 대화의 빈칸에 들어갈 말이 바르게 짝지어진 것은?

A: __________ the store opened the door?
B: No, it __________ opened the door yet.

① Have - has

② Has - has

③ Has - hasn't

④ Did - didn't

⑤ Have - haven't

11 다음 중 밑줄 친 부분이 어법상 틀린 것은?

① She has <u>kept</u> a diary.

② They <u>have</u> made dinner.

③ We have <u>never</u> eaten here.

④ I have never <u>wrote</u> a letter.

⑤ He has <u>bought</u> a new coat.

12 다음 글의 밑줄 친 부분 중 어법상 틀린 곳은?

I ①<u>have traveled</u> to many countries. Last year, I ②<u>have gone</u> to Italy and ③<u>stayed</u> for two weeks. I have always ④<u>dreamed</u> of visiting Rome, and I finally did. It ⑤<u>was</u> a memorable trip, and I hope to explore more places soon.

① ② ③ ④ ⑤

[13-14] 다음 문장에서 어법상 <u>틀린</u> 곳을 찾아 바르게 고치시오.

13

I have never hear that song before.

___________ → ___________

14

Have Minsu ever seen her since last year?

___________ → ___________

15 다음 대화의 빈칸에 들어갈 말로 가장 적절한 것은?

A: Have you read the book?
B: Yes, I _________ read it twice.

① has
② had
③ will
④ must
⑤ have

[16-17] 다음 우리말에 맞도록 괄호 안의 단어들을 바르게 배열하시오.

16

그들은 아직 떠나지 않았다.
(left / they / not / have / yet / .)

→ ___________________________

17

나는 학교에 지각한 적이 결코 없다.
(I / late / never / have / been / for school / .)

→ ___________________________

18 다음 중 빈칸에 들어갈 말로 가장 적절한 것은?

They are not here. They _________ on a school trip.

① go
② will go
③ have gone
④ has gone
⑤ went

 다음 우리말에 맞도록 빈칸에 알맞은 말을 보기 에서 골라 쓰시오.

보기 since   before   ago   after

19

그는 한 시간 전에 사무실을 떠났다.

→ He left the office an hour ______________.

20

나는 전에 그 식당에 가 본 적이 없다.

→ I have never been to that restaurant ______________.

21

다음 대화에서 어법상 <u>틀린</u> 곳을 찾아 바르게 고치시오.

A: Have you heard from her?
B: No, I haven't heard from her after last week.

______________ → ______________

22

다음 중 현재완료형이 바르게 사용된 문장을 <u>모두</u> 고르면?

① They has finished their lunch.
② I have read this novel before.
③ We had done our homework last night.
④ She has gone to the gym in the morning.
⑤ She has worked here for nine years.

23

다음 글의 밑줄 친 부분 중 어법상 옳은 것끼리 바르게 짝지어진 것은?

I ⓐ<u>have visited</u> my grandparents last weekend. We ⓑ<u>had</u> a great time together. I ⓒ<u>played</u> games with my cousins and we ⓓ<u>have gone</u> for a walk in the park. Since then, I ⓔ<u>have talked</u> to my grandparents on the phone a few times. I planned to visit them again next month.

① ⓐ
② ⓐ, ⓑ
③ ⓒ, ⓓ
④ ⓑ, ⓒ, ⓓ
⑤ ⓑ, ⓒ, ⓔ

6

to 부정사

to 부정사(to + 동사원형)의 명사적 용법 1

역할	의미	예문
주어	~하는 것은(이)	To learn a new language is exciting.
목적어	~하는 것을	She wants to travel the world.

A 다음 괄호 안에서 알맞은 것을 고르시오.

1 (Play / To play) the piano is fun.

2 She decided (go / to go) to the ocean.

to 부정사의 명사적 용법 2

역할	의미	예문
보어	~하는 것(이다)	Her dream is to become a teacher.
의문사 + to 부정사	what to: 무엇을 ~할지 how to: 어떻게 ~할지 where to: 어디서(로) ~할지 when to: 언제 ~할지 who to: 누가(누구를) ~할지	What to do next is not clear. I don't know how to solve this problem. Where to go is not important.

B 다음 괄호 안에서 알맞은 것을 고르시오.

1 His job is (fixes / to fix) the car.

2 He taught me (what to / how to) swim.

역할	의미	예문
앞의 명사 수식	~할, ~하는	I have a book to read. I need a pen to write with. <주의> 수식 받는 명사가 'to 부정사 + 전치사'의 목적어인 경우 전치사는 생략하면 안 됨(→ write with a pen)
be to 용법	예정: ~할 예정이다	He is to leave tomorrow.
	의무: ~해야 한다	You are to finish your work by noon.
	운명: ~할 운명이다	The child is to become a doctor.
	의도: ~하려고 하다	If you are to succeed, you must work hard.

C 다음 중 옳은 문장에 동그라미 하시오.

1 He has a letter to read.　　　( )

He has a letter reads.　　　( )

2 We need someone to talk.　　( )

We need someone to talk with.　( )

to 부정사의 부사적 용법

역할	의미	예문
부사 (동사, 형용사, 부사 수식)	목적: ~하기 위해, ~하러	He studied hard to pass the exam.
	감정의 원인: ~해서, ~하니	I am happy to see you again.
	결과: ~해서 (결국) ~하다	He grew up to be a famous singer.
	판단의 근거, 이유: ~하다니, ~하는 것을 보니	He must be smart to solve the problem.

D 다음 문장이 자연스럽게 이어지도록 연결하시오.

1 I study English　　　　　•　　　　• ⓐ to stay healthy.

2 He exercises regularly　•　　　　• ⓑ to trust everyone.

3 She must be foolish　　•　　　　• ⓒ to make foreign friends.

A 다음 문장에서 to 부정사를 찾아 밑줄 치시오. (없으면 X 표시하시오.)

1 I need to buy groceries.   (   )

2 We love to watch movies.   (   )

3 I am going to the store.   (   )

4 She decided to start a new project.   (   )

5 To eat vegetables is good for health.   (   )

6 To run every day keeps you healthy.   (   )

7 We are traveling to Paris next week.   (   )

8 To read books expands your knowledge.   (   )

B 다음 괄호 안에서 알맞은 것을 고르시오.

1 His idea is (writes / to write) a novel.

2 My job is (to plans / to plan) the event.

3 The aim is to (increase / increasing) sales.

4 The rule is (respects / to respect) others.

5 What (eating / to eat) is not important.

6 She showed me how (to solve / solve) the puzzle.

7 (What / How) to cook a perfect steak is not easy.

8 What do you need? You didn't tell me (how / what) to bring.

 다음 우리말에 맞도록 괄호 안의 단어들을 이용하여 문장을 완성하시오.

1 그는 운전할 차를 샀다. (drive, a car)

→ He bought _______________________________.

2 그녀는 공부할 책이 필요하다. (a book, study)

→ She needs _______________________________.

3 나는 아침 식사로 먹을 무언가가 필요하다. (eat, something)

→ I need _______________________________ for breakfast.

4 그는 올해 그 팀에 합류하려고 한다. (be, join)

→ He _______________________________ the team this year.

5 그 회의는 오전 9시에 시작될 예정이다. (be, start)

→ The meeting _______________________________ at 9 a.m.

6 너는 금요일까지 그 보고서를 끝내야 한다. (be, finish)

→ You _______________________________ the report by Friday.

D **다음 밑줄 친 부분을 괄호 안의 용법에 유의하여 우리말로 해석하시오.**

1 She wore a jacket <u>to keep warm</u>. (목적)

→ 그녀는 _______________________________ 재킷을 입었다.

2 She studied hard, only <u>to fail the exam</u>. (결과)

→ 그녀는 열심히 공부했지만, _______________________________.

3 I was surprised <u>to hear the news</u>. (감정의 원인)

→ 나는 _______________________________ 놀랐다.

4 You must be strong <u>to lift that box</u>. (판단의 근거)

→ 당신은 _______________________________ 힘이 센 것이 틀림없다.

5 He woke up early <u>to realize it was a Saturday</u>. (결과)

→ 그는 일찍 일어났는데, _______________________________.

A 다음 문장에서 to 부정사가 명사적 용법으로 쓰였으면 ○, 형용사적 용법으로 쓰였으면 △를 표시하시오.

1 I have a plan to follow. (　)

2 I want to meet with you. (　)

3 He loves to read novels. (　)

4 I need a program to use. (　)

5 She needs to go shopping. (　)

6 We hope to travel together. (　)

7 I need someone to help me. (　)

8 We need an idea to discuss. (　)

9 His task is to clean the house. (　)

10 She has something to show you. (　)

11 The answer is to study harder. (　)

12 They found a solution to apply. (　)

13 She wants someone to talk with. (　)

14 They found a way to save money. (　)

15 He found a place to park his car. (　)

16 My hope is to learn a new language. (　)

17 We need a coach to train the team. (　)

18 How to study effectively is very important. (　)

19 She brought a book to read during the trip. (　)

20 What to wear is always a challenge in winter. (　)

B 다음 문장을 괄호 안의 쓰임에 유의하여 우리말로 해석하시오.

예정: ~할 예정이다 | 의무: ~해야 한다 | 운명: ~할 운명이다 | 의도: ~하려고 하다

1   The train is to leave at noon. (예정)

→ ____

2   The concert is to begin in 30 minutes. (예정)

→ ____

3   The flight is to depart at 6 p.m. (예정)

→ ____

4   The movie is to come out next week. (예정)

→ ____

5   The event is to take place in the main hall. (예정)

→ ____

6   They are to clean the office after work. (의무)

→ ____

7   He is to attend the meeting without fail. (의무)

→ ____

8   We are to follow the instructions carefully. (의무)

→ ____

9   You are to arrive on time for the interview. (의무)

→ ____

10   The employee is to submit the form by the deadline. (의무)

→ ____

11   She is to be a leader in her field. (운명)

→ ____

12   He is to become a famous musician. (운명)

→ ____

13   If we are to catch the train, we need to leave now. (의도)

→ ____

14   If she is to become a doctor, she has to study harder. (의도)

→ ____

C 다음 괄호 안에서 알맞은 것을 고르시오.

1   She has a friend (call / to call).

2   He was thrilled (be / to be) on stage.

3   I need a moment (thinking / to think).

4   I bought a blanket (keep / to keep) warm.

5   I bought a map (finds / to find) my way.

6   We left early (avoid / to avoid) the traffic.

7   Mr. Kim has a lesson (teach / to teach).

8   I have someone (visit / to visit) later today.

9   We went on a diet (gets / to get) healthier.

10   She went to the gym (losing / to lose) weight.

11   She was proud (achieve / to achieve) her goals.

12   I turned off the light (save / to save) electricity.

13   I was thankful (have / to have) kind friends.

14   They were happy (spend / to spend) time together.

15   He was shocked (see / to see) the accident.

16   We need some space (studying / to study).

17   She has a gift (wrap / to wrap).

18   He found someone (to go / to go with).

19   She needs a notebook (to write / to write on).

20   I need a chair (to sit / to sit on).

 다음 대화의 괄호 안에서 알맞은 것을 고르시오.

1 A: We need a computer to (work / work on).

   B: OK. I'll bring one (to / for) use.

2 A: When is the party (begin / to begin)?

   B: The party (is / is to) begin at 7 p.m.

3 A: She has a document (to sign / signing).

   B: I'll help her with that task (to / for) complete.

4 A: I'm planning (to / for) go to the beach tomorrow.

   B: That sounds great! I'm excited (to / for) join you.

5 A: I am (paid / to pay) the bill today.

   B: I see. I will (pay / to pay) mine soon.

6 A: I haven't brought a notebook to (write / write on).

   B: I'll get one (to / for) you.

7 A: The hero (is / will) to defeat the villain.

   B: The hero will need courage to (defeat / defeating) him.

8 A: Can you tell me (what to / where to) get a taxi?

   B: Sure! I'll show you where to (find / finding) one.

9 A: Do you know how to (bake / baked) a cake?

   B: Yes, I do. I can show you how (made / to make) one.

10 A: Can you explain how to (use / used) this app?

   B: Sure! Let me show you how to (install / installing) it.

A 다음 우리말에 맞도록 괄호 안의 단어를 이용하여 빈칸에 알맞은 말을 쓰시오.

1 그는 불어를 배우는 것을 원한다. (learn)

→ He wants _____________ _____________ French.

2 목표는 낭비를 줄이는 것이다. (reduce)

→ The goal _____________ _____________ _____________ waste.

3 책을 쓰는 것은 시간이 걸린다. (write)

→ _____________ _____________ a book takes time.

4 내 꿈은 가게를 여는 것이다. (open)

→ My dream _____________ _____________ _____________ a store.

5 그는 의사가 되기를 바란다. (become)

→ He hopes _____________ _____________ a doctor.

6 분명하게 말하는 것은 중요하다. (speak)

→ _____________ _____________ clearly is important.

7 그들은 박물관에 방문하기로 계획한다. (visit)

→ They plan _____________ _____________ the museum.

8 내 제안은 휴식을 취하는 것이다. (take)

→ My suggestion _____________ _____________ _____________ a break.

9 다른 사람을 돕는 것은 당신을 행복하게 만든다. (help)

→ _____________ _____________ others makes you happy.

10 세계를 여행하는 것은 나의 꿈이다. (travel)

→ _____________ _____________ the world is my dream.

11 새로운 언어를 배우는 것은 신나는 일이다. (learn)

→ _____________ _____________ new languages is exciting.

12 그녀의 임무는 부엌을 치우는 것이었다. (clean)

→ Her task _____________ _____________ _____________ the kitchen.

1 오늘 밤 TV에서 무엇을 볼지는 딜레마이다.

→ _____________ _____________ watch on TV tonight is a dilemma.

2 나는 면접을 보러 어디로 가야 할지 확실치 않다.

→ I'm not sure _____________ _____________ go for the interview.

3 나는 그 프로젝트를 어떻게 시작해야 할지 모르겠다.

→ I don't know _____________ _____________ start the project.

4 그 상황에서 무엇을 말할지는 어렵다.

→ _____________ _____________ say in that situation is difficult.

5 점심으로 무엇을 먹을지는 큰 문제이다.

→ _____________ _____________ eat for lunch is the big question.

6 언제 학교를 떠날지 나에게 알려 줘.

→ Let me know _____________ _____________ leave the school.

7 나는 파리에서 어디에 머물지 모르겠다.

→ I don't know _____________ _____________ stay in Paris.

8 우리는 언제 회의를 시작할지 결정해야 한다.

→ We should decide _____________ _____________ start the meeting.

9 나는 응급 상황에서 누구에게 전화할지 모르겠다.

→ I don't know _____________ _____________ call in an emergency.

10 요즘은 누구를 믿어야 할지 알기가 어렵다.

→ It's hard to know _____________ _____________ trust these days.

11 그녀는 도시의 어디에서 자원봉사를 해야 할지 알고 싶어 한다.

→ She wants to know _____________ _____________ volunteer in the city.

12 이 방정식을 푸는 방법은 그 강좌의 주제이다.

→ _____________ _____________ solve this equation is the topic of the course.

C 다음 괄호 안의 단어들을 바르게 배열하시오.

1 (I / a place / to stay / found / .)

→ ____

2 (I / to visit / need / a website / .)

→ ____

3 (a chair / she / on / has / to sit / .)

→ ____

4 (on time / to be / a good habit / is / .) (to 부정사가 주어)

→ ____

5 (yourself / is / important / to love / .)

→ ____

6 (want / they / to go / to the beach / .)

→ ____

7 (I / to finish / hope / the task / .)

→ ____

8 (plan to / we / our website / improve / .)

→ ____

9 (to a new city / she / to move / decided / .)

→ ____

10 (can / rewards / bring / to take risks / .)

→ ____

11 (is / to start / her idea / a new business / .) (to 부정사가 보어)

→ ____

12 (builds / to trust others / strong bonds / .)

→ ____

13 (to improve / is / his purpose / his health / .)

→ ____

14 (on your work / to focus / improves / results / .)

→ ____

15 (is / their plan / to launch / a new product / .) (to 부정사가 보어)

→ ____

D 다음 괄호 안의 단어들을 바르게 배열하시오.

1 (I / something / bought / with / to write / .)

   → ____

2 (I / to clean the house / someone / hired / .)

   → ____

3 (someone / they / to join their team / found / .)

   → ____

4 (something / they / have / to give you / .)

   → ____

5 (was excited / he / to start / his new job / .)

   → ____

6 (he / went to / to buy groceries / the store / .)

   → ____

7 (woke up early / they / the train / to catch / .)

   → ____

8 (the championship / to win / he / trained every day / .)

   → ____

9 (learn next / your decision / is / what to / .)

   → ____

10 (sure / I'm not / eat for lunch / where to / .)

   → ____

11 (buy / what to / for the picnic / tell me / .)

   → ____

12 (what to bring / we heard / to the event / .)

   → ____

13 (I / what to / study for the exam / have no idea / .)

   → ____

14 (play chess / do / how to / you know / ?)

   → ____

15 (how to make / can you / show me / a website/ ?)

   → ____

1 다음 중 to 부정사의 형태가 옳은 것은?

① to met

② to saw

③ to loves

④ to make

⑤ to seeing

2 다음 중 밑줄 친 부분이 to 부정사가 <u>아닌</u> 것은?

① I like <u>to swim</u>.

② He wants <u>to go</u>.

③ I love <u>to read</u> it.

④ She gave it <u>to them</u>.

⑤ I bought a cake <u>to share</u>.

[3-4] 다음 중 빈칸에 들어갈 말로 가장 적절한 것을 고르시오.

3

He has a lot of work to ______.

① do　　　② did

③ done　　④ does

⑤ doing

4

I need a spoon to eat ______.

① to　　　② in

③ on　　　④ for

⑤ with

[5-6] 다음 우리말에 맞도록 빈칸에 알맞은 말을 쓰시오.

5

자연을 즐기는 것은 평화롭다.

→ __________ __________ nature is peaceful.

6

목표는 충분한 돈을 모으는 것이다.

→ The goal __________ __________ save enough money.

7

① His goal is to become a doctor.

② She didn't want to swim in the ocean.

③ To read books is my favorite hobby.

④ To travel the world has always been his dream.

⑤ To learning a new language can be challenging.

8

① I have a book to read.

② They have a plan to go to Jeju.

③ He is looking for a place to live in.

④ She found a restaurant to eat with.

⑤ I bought a gift to give to my friend.

[9-10] 다음 대화의 빈칸에 들어갈 말이 바르게 짝지어진 것을 고르시오.

9

A: Are you planning _______ the meeting?
B: No, I have something else _______.

① to join - to do

② joining - to do

③ to join - doing

④ join - doing

⑤ join - do

10

A: Where are you going?
B: I need _______ a pen to write _______.

① buy - on

② to buying - on

③ to buy - on

④ to buy - with

⑤ buy - with

11 다음 중 밑줄 친 부분의 쓰임이 <u>어색한</u> 것은?

① She taught me <u>how to</u> solve it.

② I know <u>how to</u> get to your place.

③ She asked me <u>where to</u> find a good hotel.

④ She asked me <u>what to</u> sit at the meeting.

⑤ He couldn't decide <u>what to</u> order for dinner.

12 다음 중 빈칸에 들어갈 말로 가장 적절한 것은?

The prince _______ marry the princess.

① to   ② was

③ was to   ④ has

⑤ has been

[13-14] 다음 문장에서 어법상 **틀린** 곳을 찾아 바르게 고치시오.

13

We brought something shares at the party.

____________ → ____________

14

To success in business, you must understand your customers' needs.

____________ → ____________

[15-16] 다음 대화의 빈칸에 들어갈 말로 가장 적절한 것을 고르시오.

15

A: I need to take a break after this meeting.
B: I see. You will need ____________.

① someone help you
② someone to help you
③ someone for help you
④ someone helping you
⑤ someone to be help you

16

A: I skipped breakfast this morning.
B: You must be really hungry.
You will want ____________.

① something eat
② to something eat
③ something for eat
④ something eating
⑤ something to eat

[17-18] 다음 우리말에 맞도록 괄호 안의 단어들을 바르게 배열하시오.

17

그 수업은 10시에 시작될 예정이다.
(at 10 o'clock / is / the class / to start / .)

→ ____________________________

18

거기에 혼자 가다니 그녀는 용감한 것이 분명해.
(she / to go / must be / there alone / brave / .)

→ ____________________________

19 다음 문장이 의미하는 것은?

The game is to begin after lunch.

① The game will begin after lunch.
② The game began before lunch.
③ The game must begin before lunch.
④ The game might not begin after lunch.
⑤ The game will not begin after lunch.

[20-21] 다음 우리말에 맞도록 빈칸에 알맞은 말을 보기 에서 골라 쓰시오.

| 보기 | to | in | with | about |

20

우리는 놀 공원을 발견했다.

→ We found a park to play _____________.

21

당신은 이야기할 새로운 주제를 찾았나요?

→ Did you find a new topic to talk
_____________?

22 다음 대화에서 쓰임이 <u>어색한</u> <u>두 곳</u>을 찾아 바르게 고치시오.

A: I'm lost. I have no idea what to
get to the station.
B: Let me check. You definitely
need a map for read.

A: _____________ → _____________

B: _____________ → _____________

23 다음 글의 밑줄 친 부분 중 어법상 옳은 것끼리 바르게 짝지어진 것은?

My dream is ⓐ<u>to become</u> a professional singer. I have a passion ⓑ<u>explore</u> things about music. I practice regularly ⓒ<u>to improve</u> my voice. I found a mentor ⓓ<u>guide</u> my journey. With each performance, I gain confidence. Someday, I hope ⓔ<u>to help</u> music lovers.

① ⓐ, ⓒ
② ⓑ, ⓓ
③ ⓐ, ⓒ, ⓔ
④ ⓐ, ⓓ, ⓔ
⑤ ⓐ, ⓑ, ⓒ, ⓔ

7

to 부정사와 동명사

- to 부정사를 이용한 구문
- to 부정사만을 목적어로 취하는 동사
- 동명사의 형태와 역할
- 동명사만을 목적어로 취하는 동사

to 부정사를 이용한 구문

구문	의미	예문
not to 동사원형	~하지 않기 위해, ~하지 않을 것을	He decided not to attend the meeting.
in order to 동사원형	~하기 위해	I woke up early in order to catch the train.
enough to 동사원형	~하기에 충분한	She is strong enough to carry the suitcase.
too (형 / 부) to 동사원형	너무 ~해서 …할 수 없다	The movie was too boring to watch.
be about to 동사원형	곧 ~하려 하다	The train is about to leave.

A 다음 두 문장의 의미가 같도록 빈칸에 알맞은 말을 쓰시오.

1 He is very strong, so he can move this heavy box.

= He is strong _______________ to move this heavy box.

2 This puzzle is very difficult, so we can't solve it easily.

= This puzzle is _______________ difficult to solve easily.

to 부정사만을 목적어로 취하는 동사

동사	예문
want, hope, wish, desire, plan, expect, decide, ask, need, manage, fail, seem, refuse, promise, choose 등	I want to finish the project today. He seems to be tired.
enable, allow, tell, invite + 목적어 + to 부정사	The teacher enabled the students to understand the lesson better.

B 다음 괄호 안에서 알맞은 것을 고르시오.

1 I hope (traveling / to travel) to Europe next year.

2 She told me (wait / to wait) in the lobby.

3 They allow us (using / to use) the library after class.

형태	역할	예문
동사 + ing	주어	Reading books is enjoyable. (책을 <u>읽는 것</u>은 즐겁다.)
	목적어	I enjoy reading. (나는 <u>읽기</u>를 즐긴다.)
	보어	Her hobby is singing. (그녀의 취미는 <u>노래하기</u>이다.)

C 다음 괄호 안에서 알맞은 것을 고르시오.

1 (Swim / Swimming) is fun.

2 My job is (teaching / teach) English.

동명사만을 목적어로 취하는 동사

동사	예문
enjoy, keep, practice, finish, give up, quit, mind, avoid, admit, deny, postpone, delay, put off 등	I enjoy playing tennis. She finished writing the book. He avoids using his phone at night.

to 부정사와 동명사를 모두 취하는 기본 동사들
좋아하고(like, love, prefer), 싫어하고(hate), 시작하는(begin, start) 동사들

D 다음 중 옳은 문장에 동그라미 하시오.

1 I enjoy to sing songs.   (   )

I enjoy singing songs.   (   )

2 He gave up playing soccer.   (   )

He gave up play soccer.   (   )

A 다음 우리말에 맞도록 빈칸에 알맞은 말을 쓰시오.

1 해가 곧 지려 한다.

→ The sun is ______________ to set.

2 나는 곧 집을 떠나려 한다.

→ I am ______________ to leave the house.

3 그 아이는 너무 약해서 걸을 수 없었다.

→ The child was ______________ weak to walk.

4 그는 새 차를 살 만큼 충분히 부유하다.

→ He is rich ______________ to buy a new car.

5 그 소설은 너무 길어서 읽을 수 없었다.

→ The novel was ______________ long to read.

6 그는 선명하게 보기 위해 안경을 썼다.

→ He wore glasses in ______________ to see clearly.

7 그녀는 살을 빼기 위해 매일 운동했다.

→ She exercised every day in ______________ to lose weight.

8 그들은 마감 기한을 넘기지 않기 위해 늦게까지 일했다.

→ They worked late ______________ to miss the deadline.

B 다음 괄호 안에서 알맞은 것을 고르시오.

1 I asked (leave / to leave) early.

2 She told me to (call / calling) her.

3 He chose (to study / studying) biology.

4 Mike decided (go / to go) for a walk.

5 Mia wishes (traveling / to travel) the world.

6 Sam desires (to learn / learning) new languages.

7 He expects (hearing / to hear) from her soon.

C 다음 우리말에 맞도록 빈칸에 알맞은 말을 보기 에서 골라 쓰시오. (필요시 어형을 바꾸되, 한 단어로 쓸 것)

보기 paint   write   read   swim   sing

1 나는 수영하는 것을 즐긴다.

→ I enjoy ____________.

2 글쓰기는 중요하다.

→ ____________ is important.

3 그의 재능은 노래하는 것이다.

→ His talent is ____________.

4 읽기는 당신이 배우는 데 도움이 된다.

→ ____________ helps you learn.

5 그는 풍경화 그리는 것을 좋아한다.

→ He likes ____________ landscapes.

D 다음 우리말에 맞도록 빈칸에 알맞은 말을 보기 에서 골라 쓰시오. (필요시 어형을 바꿀 것)

보기 practice   quit   mind   keep   finish

1 나는 너를 기다리는 것을 신경쓰지 않는다.

→ I don't ____________ waiting for you.

2 그는 매일 노래 부르는 것을 연습한다.

→ He ____________ singing every day.

3 그는 시험공부를 계속한다.

→ He ____________ studying for the exam.

4 그들은 집 청소를 끝냈다.

→ They ____________ cleaning the house.

5 어머니는 곧 일을 그만두실지도 모른다.

→ My mother may ____________ her job soon.

A 다음 괄호 안의 우리말에 맞도록 빈칸에 알맞은 말을 보기 에서 골라 쓰시오.

보기   too   about   enough   not   order

1 I am ___________ to call her. (곧 전화하려 하다)

2 She smiled ___________ to look sad. (~하게 보이지 않기 위해)

3 She left early ___________ to miss the bus. (놓치지 않기 위해)

4 The train is ___________ to leave. (곧 떠나려 하다)

5 The box was ___________ big to fit in. (너무 커서 ~할 수 없었다)

6 The car is fast ___________ to race. (~하기에 충분히 빠르다)

7 The soup was ___________ hot to drink. (너무 뜨거워서 ~할 수 없었다)

8 The meeting is ___________ to begin. (곧 시작하려 하다)

9 The test was easy ___________ to pass. (~하기에 충분히 쉬웠다)

10 The plane is ___________ to land. (곧 착륙하려 하다)

11 I am studying ___________ to fail the exam. (실패하지 않기 위해)

12 I took notes ___________ to forget the details. (잊지 않기 위해)

13 He raised his hand in ___________ to ask a question. (물어보기 위해)

14 She was ___________ young to attend the event. (너무 어려서 ~할 수 없었다)

15 She was brave ___________ to speak in public. (~하기에 충분히 용감했다)

16 He packed his bag in ___________ to leave quickly. (떠나기 위해)

17 He was ___________ tired to continue the work. (너무 피곤해서 ~할 수 없었다)

18 We arrived early in ___________ to prepare the play. (준비하기 위해)

19 The suit is cheap ___________ to buy right now. (~하기에 충분히 싸다)

1   Mom encouraged me (to try / trying) again.

2   She quit (to work / working) at the company.

3   They keep (to work / working) on the project.

4   They don't mind (to travel / traveling) for work.

5   Sally wished (to meet / meeting) him in person.

6   We practice (to write / writing) essays regularly.

7   My uncle expects (to get / getting) the job soon.

8   He hopes (to finish / finishing) his work by 5 p.m.

9   I want (to learn / learning) how to play the guitar.

10   My father enjoys (to fish / fishing) in the winter.

11   She seems (be / to be) very busy these days.

12   They told us (being / to be) on time.

13   He wishes (to improve / improving) his English skills.

14   We expect (to learn / learning) a lot in this course.

15   She hopes (to join / joining) the team next season.

16   Mr. Lee allowed us (using / to use) laptops during the test.

17   Julie wants (to visit / visiting) her family next month.

18   The lecture enabled him (improve / to improve) his scores.

19   The young man denied (to steal / stealing) the money.

20   My brothers avoid (to watch / watching) violent movies.

C 다음 괄호 안의 단어를 알맞은 형태로 바꿔 빈칸에 쓰시오.

1   I expect ____________ in a big city. (live)

2   She denied ____________ the vase. (break)

3   Jake put off ____________ to the gym. (go)

4   He invited me ____________ the team. (join)

5   She wishes ____________ him again. (meet)

6   He admitted ____________ on the test. (cheat)

7   My mom planned ____________ her job. (quit)

8   They delayed ____________ the restaurant. (leave)

9   The meeting seems ____________ going well. (be)

10   I desire ____________ in a peaceful village. (live)

11   He failed ____________ the report on time. (submit)

12   She asked ____________ with the manager. (speak)

13   Mr. Baek postponed ____________ a restaurant. (open)

14   He managed ____________ the problem quickly. (solve)

15   Jihyun keeps ____________ to improve her skills. (try)

16   They told him ____________ immediately. (leave)

17   I failed ____________ the book before the deadline. (finish)

18   This tool enables you ____________ tasks easily. (perform)

19   This spot seems ____________ attractive to many tourists. (be)

20   They allowed us ____________ a picture in the museum. (take)

 다음 대화의 괄호 안에서 알맞은 것을 고르시오.

1   A: He managed (to fix / fixing) the broken phone.

    B: That's great! Did he enjoy (to help / helping) you with that?

2   A: Did you finish (to read / reading) that book?

    B: Yes, I decided (to start / starting) a new one right away.

3   A: Do you mind (to turn / turning) off the TV?

    B: Not at all. I was just about (to switch / switching) it off anyway.

4   A: We plan (to go / going) on vacation next month.

    B: Good! We need (to save / saving) enough money for a trip, then.

5   A: He decided (to stop / stopping) drinking coffee.

    B: Really? He really enjoyed (to have / having) a cup every morning.

6   A: Why do you keep (to check / checking) your phone?

    B: I'm waiting (to hear / hearing) from my friend.

7   A: Do you want (to visit / visiting) this museum again?

    B: Yes, I hope (to see / seeing) it more thoroughly next time.

8   A: She promised (to bake / baking) a cake for me.

    B: Wow, she really enjoys (to bake / baking).

9   A: I won't give up (to learn / learning) Spanish.

    B: That's great! Keep (to practice / practicing) and you'll improve.

10 A: Did you admit (to break / breaking) the vase?

    B: Yes, I decided (to apologize / apologizing) immediately.

A 다음 우리말에 맞도록 빈칸에 알맞은 말을 쓰시오.

1 콘서트가 곧 시작하려 한다.
   → The concert ___________ ___________ ___________ start.

2 그 수프는 먹기에 충분히 뜨겁다.
   → The soup is ___________ ___________ ___________ eat.

3 그 책은 사기에는 너무 비쌌다.
   → The book was ___________ expensive ___________ ___________.

4 그녀는 감기에 걸리지 않으려고 코트를 입었다.
   → She wore a coat ___________ ___________ catch a cold.

5 그는 버스를 잡아타기에 충분히 빨랐다.
   → He was quick ___________ ___________ catch the bus.

6 그 차는 제대로 달리기에는 너무 낡았다.
   → The car was ___________ ___________ ___________ run properly.

7 그는 회의에 참석하기에는 너무 아팠다.
   → He was ___________ ___________ ___________ attend the meeting.

8 그녀는 곧 그녀의 발표를 시작하려 한다.
   → She ___________ ___________ ___________ start her presentation.

9 그녀는 더 잘 듣기 위해 더 가까이 움직였다.
   → She moved closer ___________ ___________ ___________ hear better.

10 그 물은 샤워하기에 충분히 따뜻하다.
   → The water is warm ___________ ___________ take a shower.

11 그녀는 면접에 늦지 않기 위해 빨리 달렸다.
   → She ran quickly ___________ ___________ ___________ late for the interview.

12 그들은 더 나은 일자리를 찾기 위해 도시로 이사했다.
   → They moved to the city ___________ ___________ ___________ find better jobs.

 다음 우리말에 맞도록 괄호 안의 단어를 알맞은 형태로 바꿔 쓰시오

1 나는 새로운 취미를 시작하기로 결심했다. (start)

→ I decided ＿＿＿＿＿＿ a new hobby.

2 그들은 정크 푸드를 먹는 것을 피한다. (eat)

→ They avoid ＿＿＿＿＿＿ junk food.

3 그녀는 새로운 요리하는 것을 즐긴다. (cook)

→ She enjoys ＿＿＿＿＿＿ new food.

4 그는 피트니스 클럽에 가입할 계획이다. (join)

→ He plans ＿＿＿＿＿＿ the fitness club.

5 김 선생님은 그에게 말하는 것을 멈추라고 말했다. (stop)

→ Mr. Kim told him ＿＿＿＿＿＿ talking.

6 우리는 그가 용기를 내어 말하도록 격려했다. (speak)

→ We encouraged him ＿＿＿＿＿＿ up.

7 나는 제시간에 시험을 마쳤다. (take)

→ I finished ＿＿＿＿＿＿ the test on time.

8 그들은 버스를 기다리는 것을 포기했다. (wait)

→ They gave up ＿＿＿＿＿＿ for the bus.

9 그녀는 주말마다 그림을 연습한다. (draw)

→ She practices ＿＿＿＿＿＿ every weekend.

10 그는 역사에 대해 많이 알고 있는 것 같다. (know)

→ He seems ＿＿＿＿＿＿ a lot about history.

11 그 장학금 덕분에 나는 대학에 다닐 수 있었다. (attend)

→ The scholarship enabled me ＿＿＿＿＿＿ college.

12 그 규정은 직원들이 재택근무하는 것을 허용한다. (work)

→ The rules allow employees ＿＿＿＿＿＿ from home.

C 다음 괄호 안의 단어들을 바르게 배열하시오.

1 (is / playing / games / exciting / .)
→ ______________________________________

2 (is / painting / her passion / .)
→ ______________________________________

3 (cooking / a useful skill / is / .)
→ ______________________________________

4 (makes / singing / me / happy / .)
→ ______________________________________

5 (healthy / keeps / you / jogging / .)
→ ______________________________________

6 (I / my job / quitting / consider / .)
→ ______________________________________

7 (she / homework / doing / hates / .)
→ ______________________________________

8 (is / hobby / my favorite / dancing / .) (동명사가 주어)
→ ______________________________________

9 (at the lake / very relaxing / is / fishing / .)
→ ______________________________________

10 (activity / my favorite / reading / is / .) (동명사가 보어)
→ ______________________________________

11 (is / interest / cooking / their main / .) (동명사가 보어)
→ ______________________________________

12 (broadens / traveling / your mind / .)
→ ______________________________________

13 (cooking dinner / loves / my father / .)
→ ______________________________________

14 (her / playing the violin / is / specialty / .) (동명사가 보어)
→ ______________________________________

15 (important / setting / is / his objective / .) (동명사가 주어)
→ ______________________________________

D 다음 괄호 안의 단어들을 바르게 배열하시오.

1 (he / taking / delayed / the exam / .)

→ ______________________________________

2 (the money / she / taking / denied / .)

→ ______________________________________

3 (I / lying / to my friend / admitted / .)

→ ______________________________________

4 (deciding / we / put off / the menu / .)

→ ______________________________________

5 (she / a new job / looking for / quit / .)

→ ______________________________________

6 (I / going / avoid / to crowded places / .)

→ ______________________________________

7 (in the ocean / enjoy / polar bears / swimming / .)

→ ______________________________________

8 (we / a mistake / making / admitted / .)

→ ______________________________________

9 (I / thinking / keep / about the decision / .)

→ ______________________________________

10 (hiking / enjoys / he / in the mountains / .)

→ ______________________________________

11 (considered / he / changing / his career / .)

→ ______________________________________

12 (I / don't / cooking / mind / dinner tonight / .)

→ ______________________________________

13 (he / running / practices / every morning / .)

→ ______________________________________

14 (finished / we / the homework / doing / .)

→ ______________________________________

15 (didn't / math / she / studying / give up / .)

→ ______________________________________

1 다음 중 빈칸에 들어갈 말로 가장 적절한 것은?

His hobby is ____________ chess.

① play ② plays
③ played ④ playing
⑤ has played

2 다음 중 빈칸에 들어갈 말로 적절한 것을 <u>모두</u> 고르면?

____________ takes time.

① Learn ② Learns
③ Learned ④ Learning
⑤ To learn

3 다음 중 to 부정사를 목적어로 취하지 <u>않는</u> 동사는?

① want
② hope
③ enjoy
④ wish
⑤ desire

4 다음 중 to 부정사와 동명사를 모두 목적어로 취할 수 있는 동사가 <u>아닌</u> 것은?

① like
② avoid
③ love
④ hate
⑤ begin

5 다음 중 밑줄 친 부분의 쓰임이 나머지와 <u>다른</u> 것은?

① <u>Cooking</u> dinner is fun.
② Their passion is <u>acting</u>.
③ My dog is <u>waiting</u> for me.
④ <u>Singing</u> brings people together.
⑤ Our mission is <u>solving</u> the issue.

[6-7] 다음 우리말에 맞도록 빈칸에 알맞은 말을 쓰시오.

6

그 공연이 곧 시작하려고 한다.

→ The show is ____________ to begin.

7

그는 그녀에게 아무에게도 말하지 말라고
부탁했다.

→ He asked her ＿＿＿＿＿＿ ＿＿＿＿＿＿
tell anyone.

**[8-9] 다음 두 문장의 의미가 같도록 빈칸에 알맞은
단어를 보기 에서 골라 쓰시오.**

보기 enough order too not

8

The movie was very boring, so I couldn't
enjoy it.

= The movie was ＿＿＿＿＿＿ boring to
enjoy.

9

The instructions were very clear, so we
could follow them.

= The instructions were clear ＿＿＿＿＿＿
to follow.

[10-11] 다음 중 어법상 <u>틀린</u> 것을 고르시오.

10

① I suggest to go to the beach.

② He misses traveling the world.

③ His purpose is helping others.

④ They failed to deliver it on time.

⑤ His ambition is becoming a doctor.

11

① I started reading mystery novels.

② Tim likes swimming in the ocean.

③ Jill began to work on the project.

④ She hates watching horror movies.

⑤ He considers to go back to school.

12 다음 중 빈칸에 들어갈 말로 적절하지 <u>않은</u> 것은?

He ＿＿＿＿＿ reading comic books
before dinner.

① loves

② wants

③ enjoys

④ avoids

⑤ finishes

13 다음 중 빈칸에 들어갈 말로 적절한 것을 <u>모두</u> 고르면?

> I __________ going out for lunch with my coworkers.

① enjoyed　　② promised

③ desired　　④ suggested

⑤ needed

[14-15] 다음 대화의 빈칸에 들어갈 말이 바르게 짝지어진 것을 고르시오.

14

> A: I decided __________ to a new apartment next month.
> B: Really? Have you finished __________ your boxes yet?

① to move – packing

② to move – packed

③ to move – to pack

④ moving – packing

⑤ moving – to pack

15

> A: Did you manage __________ the puzzle?
> B: Actually, I gave up __________ it.

① solve – solving

② to solve – to solve

③ to solve – solving

④ solving – solving

⑤ solving – to solve

[16-17] 다음 문장에서 어법상 <u>틀린</u> 곳을 찾아 바르게 고치시오.

16

> She seems enjoy working with her mother in the garden.

__________ → __________

17

> Reading stories often enables people see things differently.

__________ → __________

[18-19] 다음 우리말에 맞도록 괄호 안의 단어들을 바르게 배열하시오. (필요시 어형을 바꿀 것)

18

> Jimmy는 긴 줄에서 기다리는 것을 싫어한다.
> (hates / Jimmy / wait / in long lines / .)

→ __________

19

그들은 매일 저녁 축구하는 것을 연습한다.
(play / they / soccer / practice / every evening / .)

→ ____

20 다음 대화에서 어법상 <u>틀린</u> 곳을 찾아 바르게 고치시오.

A: She avoids eating sweet food these days.
B: I know. She desires living a healthier life.

____________ → ____________

[21–22] 다음 그림을 보고 괄호 안의 단어들을 이용하여 빈칸에 알맞은 말을 쓰시오.

21

(spicy, eat)

The food is ____________ ____________

____________ ____________ .

22

(hope, travel)

She ____________s ____________

____________ abroad someday.

23 다음 글의 밑줄 친 부분 중 어법상 옳은 것끼리 바르게 짝지어진 것은?

Shannon used to talk to her friend every day. One day, her friend lied to her, and Shannon decided not ⓐ<u>trusting</u> her. So, she quit ⓑ<u>talking</u> to the friend. She wanted ⓒ<u>to find</u> honest friends. She enjoyed ⓓ<u>meeting</u> new people. Now, she is happy because she has new honest friends.

① ⓐ
② ⓐ, ⓑ
③ ⓑ, ⓒ
④ ⓐ, ⓒ, ⓓ
⑤ ⓑ, ⓒ, ⓓ

8

수동태

- 수동태의 개념과 형태
- 수동태의 시제
- 수동태의 부정문과 의문문
- by 이외의 다양한 전치사

수동태의 개념과 형태

개념	능동태: 주어가 ~ 하다 수동태: 주어가 (~에 의해) ~되다
형태	능동태: 주어 + 동사 + 목적어 수동태: 주어 + (be + 과거분사) + by + 목적격

She teaches them.

They are taught by her.

<by + 행위자> 생략 가능: 일반적인 사람, 중요(분명)하지 않은 경우

<주의> 수동태로 쓰지 않는 동사
❶ 자동사(목적어가 없으므로 수동태로 사용 불가): occur, happen, disappear, exist 등
❷ 상태나 소유를 나타내는 동사: have, belong, become, resemble 등

A 다음 괄호 안의 우리말에 맞도록 빈칸에 알맞은 말을 쓰시오.

1 She writes the letter. → The letter ____________ ____________ by her.
(그 편지는 그녀에 의해 쓰인다.)

2 They build the house. → The house ____________ ____________ by them.
(그 집은 그들에 의해 지어진다.)

수동태의 시제

시제	형태	능동태 → 수동태
과거	was / were + p.p.	Mr. Kim taught the students. → The students were taught by Mr. Kim.
현재진행형	am / is / are + being + p.p.	Mr. Kim is teaching the students. → The students are being taught by Mr. Kim.
과거진행형	was / were + being + p.p.	Mr. Kim was teaching the students. → The students were being taught by Mr. Kim.
미래	will + be + p.p.	Mr. Kim will teach the students. →The students will be taught by Mr. Kim.

B 다음 괄호 안에서 알맞은 것을 고르시오.

1 The novel (is / was) read by many students these days.

2 The wall (was / were) painted by them yesterday.

3 The food will (is / be) cooked by my mother.

수동태의 부정문과 의문문		
형태	구조	예문
부정문	• 주어 + be동사 + not + p.p. + (by + 목적격) • 주어 + 조동사 + not be + p.p. + (by + 목적격)	The homework is not done by him. The homework won't be done by him.
의문문	• Be동사 + 주어 + p.p. + (by + 목적격) ~? • 조동사 + 주어 + be + p.p. + (by + 목적격) ~?	Is the homework done by him? Will the homework be done by him?

C 다음 중 옳은 문장에 동그라미 하시오.

1   The car is not wash by him.   (   )

   The car is not washed by him.   (   )

2   Is the box moved by the boy?   (   )

   Does the box moved by the boy?   (   )

by 이외의 다양한 전치사		
전치사	의미	예시
to	~에게	be given to, be known to
with	~으로, ~에	be filled with, be satisfied with
at	(특정한 상황) ~에	be surprised at, be disappointed at[with]
from, of	~로(부터)	be made from, be made of
as	~으로	be known as
in	(분야) ~에	be interested in

D 다음 대화의 괄호 안에서 알맞은 것을 고르시오.

1   A: Do you know Mr. Smith?

   B: Yes, he's known (at / as) the best teacher in the school.

2   A: Did you see the news?

   B: Yes, I was so surprised (at / of) the news.

A 다음 중 수동태 문장에는 ○, 능동태 문장에는 △를 표시하시오.

1 The maid cleans the room.   (   )

2 The book is sold worldwide.   (   )

3 The birds live by the shore.   (   )

4 The chef decorated the cake.   (   )

5 The cake is eaten every day.   (   )

6 The picture is drawn by the artist.   (   )

7 The letter is delivered in the morning.   (   )

8 The choir sings the song at the concert.   (   )

B 다음 괄호 안에서 알맞은 것을 고르시오.

1 The tree (was cut / was cutting) by the woodcutter.

2 The task (finished / was finished) by Jane yesterday.

3 The building (is / was) designed by the architect last year.

4 The movie (be / will be) watched by many people next week.

5 The presentation (is / will be) prepared by my team tomorrow.

6 The letter (was / is being) delivered by the postman last week.

7 The dishes (being / are being) washed by the machine now.

8 The document (being / is being) signed by the manager right now.

C 다음 우리말에 맞도록 괄호 안의 단어를 이용하여 빈칸에 알맞은 말을 쓰시오.

1 숙제가 아직 끝나지 않았다. (done)

→ The homework ＿＿＿＿＿ ＿＿＿＿＿ ＿＿＿＿＿ yet.

2 그 팀은 팬들에 의해 지지를 받지 못한다. (supported)

→ The team ＿＿＿＿＿ ＿＿＿＿＿ ＿＿＿＿＿ by the fans.

3 그 집은 청소부에 의해 청소되지 않는다. (cleaned)

→ The house ＿＿＿＿＿ ＿＿＿＿＿ ＿＿＿＿＿ by the cleaner.

4 그 시험은 선생님에 의해 채점되나요? (graded)

→ ＿＿＿＿＿ the test ＿＿＿＿＿ by the teacher?

5 이 제품은 전문가들에 의해 검사되나요? (tested)

→ ＿＿＿＿＿ this product ＿＿＿＿＿ by experts?

6 그 상품들은 회사에 의해 배송되나요? (shipped)

→ ＿＿＿＿＿ the goods ＿＿＿＿＿ by the company?

D 다음 우리말에 맞도록 빈칸에 들어갈 알맞은 말을 보기 에서 골라 쓰시오.

> 보기   filled with   satisfied with   surprised at   given to   known to

1 상은 우승자에게 주어졌다.

→ The prize was ＿＿＿＿＿ ＿＿＿＿＿ the winner.

2 그 바구니는 신선한 과일로 가득 차 있다.

→ The basket is ＿＿＿＿＿ ＿＿＿＿＿ fresh fruit.

3 그녀는 그 멋진 선물에 놀랐다.

→ She was ＿＿＿＿＿ ＿＿＿＿＿ the wonderful gift.

4 그녀는 자신의 프로젝트 결과에 만족하고 있다.

→ She is ＿＿＿＿＿ ＿＿＿＿＿ the results of her project.

5 그 진실은 방 안에 있는 모든 사람에게 알려졌다.

→ The truth was ＿＿＿＿＿ ＿＿＿＿＿ everyone in the room.

A 다음 중 어법상 옳은 문장에는 ○, 틀린 문장에는 X를 표시하시오

1 The event is occurred.   (   )

2 The car is parked outside.   (   )

3 The teacher grades the test.   (   )

4 A car is had by my brother.   (   )

5 The book is belonged to her.   (   )

6 The exam took by the students.   (   )

7 The song is played at every party.   (   )

8 The lessons taught by the teacher.   (   )

9 The books are read by the students.   (   )

10 The keys disappeared from the table.   (   )

11 The classroom cleaned by the janitor.   (   )

12 The project is presented by the group.   (   )

13 The solution is existed for a long time.   (   )

14 The students completed the assignment.   (   )

15 The desks are arranged by the students.   (   )

16 The papers are hand out by the teacher.   (   )

17 The news is broadcast on TV every evening.   (   )

18 The classroom are decorated by the students.   (   )

19 The announcements are made by the principal.   (   )

20 The accident is happened on the way to school.   (   )

 다음 괄호 안에서 알맞은 것을 고르시오.

1 The test (is / are) taken every Monday.

2 The articles (will be / are) written next week.

3 The flowers (will be / will) watered tomorrow.

4 The project (is / are) presented by the leader.

5 The notes (were / are being) taken right now.

6 The new rules (are / were) explained last week.

7 The car can (be / is) repaired in the afternoon.

8 The meeting (was / will) held on Tuesday.

9 The homework (is / will be) checked next Monday.

10 The invitation can (be / is) sent by the organizer.

11 The homework (is / was) being submitted right now.

12 The reports were (reviewing / reviewed) at the office.

13 The packages should (deliver / be delivered) by noon.

14 The computers (were / are being) used at the moment.

15 The contract must (write / be written) by both parties.

16 The questions (are / were) answered by them yesterday.

17 The meal is (be / being) served by the waiter at this time.

18 The school (is / was) visited by many parents last month.

19 The board game (is / was) played every weekend.

20 My writing (is being / was) corrected by Ms. Sally last night.

C 다음 대화의 괄호 안에서 알맞은 것을 고르시오.

1 A: Is the project (started / starting) by the manager?
   B: Yes, it (does start / is started) by the manager.

2 A: Is the movie (directed / direct) by the filmmaker?
   B: Yes, it is (directed / directing) by the filmmaker.

3 A: (Is / Was) the team coached by the trainer last year?
   B: No, the trainer (didn't train / was trained) them.

4 A: Is the task (assigned / assigning) by the boss?
   B: Yes, the task (is assigned / assigns) by him.

5 A: (Did / Was) the technician make the repairs?
   B: No, the repairs (didn't make / were not made) by him.

6 A: Did the engineer (solve / solved) the problem?
   B: Yes, the problem (has / was) solved by the engineer.

7 A: Was the speech (gave / given) by the president?
   B: No, it (wasn't / didn't).

8 A: Was the office (decorated / decorating) by the designer?
   B: Yes, it (did / was).

9 A: (Did / Were) the library books returned by them yesterday?
   B: No, the library books (didn't / were not) returned yesterday.

10 A: (Are / Were) the clothes ironed by the housekeeper yesterday?
    B: No, the clothes (were not ironed / didn't iron) by her.

 다음 우리말에 맞도록 빈칸에 알맞은 단어를 보기 에서 골라 쓰시오.

보기　　as　　by　　in　　of　　to　　from　　at　　with

1 그 상자는 판지로 만들어졌다.

→ The box is made ___________ cardboard.

2 와인은 포도로 만들어진다.

→ Wine is made ___________ grapes.

3 그 방은 웃음소리로 가득 차 있다.

→ The room is filled ___________ laughter.

4 그녀는 재능 있는 가수로 알려져 있다.

→ She is known ___________ a talented singer.

5 규칙은 모두에 의해 지켜진다.

→ The rules are followed ___________ everyone.

6 나는 역사책을 읽는 데 관심이 있다.

→ I am interested ___________ reading history books.

7 그 상은 최고의 학생에게 주어졌다.

→ The award was given ___________ the best student.

8 그 결정은 지금 대중에게 알려졌다.

→ The decision is known ___________ the public now.

9 몇몇 학생들은 자신의 성적에 만족하고 있다.

→ Some students are satisfied ___________ their grades.

10 이 책은 문학에서 고전으로 알려져 있다.

→ This book is known ___________ a classic in literature.

11 나는 예상치 못한 시험 결과에 놀랐다.

→ I was surprised ___________ the unexpected test results.

A 다음 괄호 안의 단어들을 바르게 배열하여 문장을 완성하시오.

1 (was / the room / painted)

→ _________________________________ by me.

2 (are / prepared / the meals)

→ _________________________________ by my father.

3 (sent / the invitation / was)

→ _________________________________ by the organizer.

4 (the questions / answered / are)

→ _________________________________ by the students.

5 (pointed / their mistakes / are)

→ _________________________________ out by the manager.

6 (the homework / checked / being / is)

→ _________________________________ by my mom.

7 (was / the project / completed)

→ _________________________________ together by the team.

8 (will / the reports / prepared / be)

→ _________________________________ by the director.

9 (are / the plans / being / processed)

→ _________________________________ by the clerk.

10 (being / the job / done / was)

→ _________________________________ all night by the team.

11 (will / the results / be / not)

→ _________________________________ published.

12 (the documents / not / are / filed)

→ _________________________________ properly.

13 (wasn't / the meeting / planned)

→ _________________________________ for the next day.

14 (not / the files / transferred / were)

→ _________________________________ to the system.

15 (cleaned / is / the room)

→ _________________________________ every day?

B 다음 문장을 수동태로 바꿔 쓰시오.

1 She bought groceries.

→ ____

2 The police caught the thief.

→ ____

3 They took a wrong turn.

→ ____

4 They built a new playground.

→ ____

5 He found the answer to the question.

→ ____

6 He didn't love the movie.

→ ____

7 She didn't write the email.

→ ____

8 The convenience store doesn't sell books.

→ ____

C 다음 문장을 능동태로 바꿔 쓰시오.

1 An apple is eaten by her.

→ ____

2 The movie was seen by us.

→ ____

3 A gift is given to her friend by her.

→ ____

4 Their house was sold last year by them.

→ ____

5 His mother is called every evening by him.

→ ____

6 We were not helped by them.

→ ____

D 다음 우리말에 맞도록 괄호 안의 단어를 이용하여 빈칸에 알맞은 말을 쓰시오.

1 그 문은 밤에 잠겨 있다. (lock)

→ The door ___________ ___________ at night.

2 그 학교는 매일 밤 청소된다. (clean)

→ The school ___________ ___________ every night.

3 커피는 그녀에 의해 우리에게 제공되지 않는다. (serve)

→ Coffee ___________ ___________ ___________ to us by her.

4 그 케이크는 그들에 의해 파티에서 먹혔다. (eat)

→ The cake ___________ ___________ at the party by them.

5 그 학생들은 어제 그에 의해 불렸다. (call)

→ The students ___________ ___________ yesterday by him.

6 따뜻한 환대가 그에게 주어졌다. (give)

→ A warm welcome ___________ ___________ to him.

7 그 이메일들은 어제 보내지지 않았다. (send)

→ The emails ___________ ___________ ___________ yesterday.

8 그녀는 아무에게도 숙제를 도움받지 않았다. (help)

→ She ___________ ___________ ___________ with homework by anyone.

9 그 책들은 사서에 의해 분류되고 있다. (sort)

→ The books ___________ ___________ ___________ by the librarian.

10 그 프로젝트는 그 팀에 의해 진행되고 있다. (work)

→ The project ___________ ___________ ___________ on by the team.

11 그 주제가 논의되고 있었다. (discuss)

→ The topic ___________ ___________ ___________ .

12 그 건물은 작년에 보수 중이었다. (renovate)

→ The building ___________ ___________ ___________ last year.

13 내가 들어갔을 때 그 편지는 쓰여지고 있었다. (write)

→ The letter ___________ ___________ ___________ when I entered.

14 그 계약서는 양 당사자에 의해 서명되었나요? (sign)

→ ___________ the contract ___________ ___________ both parties?

15 그 벽들이 지금 페인트로 칠해지고 있나요? (paint)

→ ___________ the walls ___________ ___________ right now?

E 다음 괄호 안의 단어들을 바르게 배열하시오.

1 (seen / she / by anyone / is / not / .)

→ ____

2 (made / a sandwich / by the chef / is / .)

→ ____

3 (found / her keys / by her / were / .)

→ ____

4 (interested / is / he / in joining / the football team / .)

→ ____

5 (made / the furniture / not / from / is / wood / .)

→ ____

6 (bought / a new car / by us / was / .)

→ ____

7 (published / the book / in 2005 / was / .)

→ ____

8 (sold / the shoes / last year / were / not / .)

→ ____

9 (given / the book / to me / was / the teacher / by / .)

→ ____

10 (being completed / the task / by the boss / was / .)

→ ____

11 (being served / the customers / are / by the staff / .)

→ ____

12 (delivered / was / the package / yesterday / ?)

→ ____

13 (watched / is / the movie / by a lot of people / ?)

→ ____

14 (posted / the exam results / online / will / be / .)

→ ____

15 (followed / the schedule / should / be / by all members / .)

→ ____

1 다음 중 수동태로 사용할 수 <u>없는</u> 동사는?

① eat

② see

③ give

④ make

⑤ belong

2 다음 중 수동태를 사용한 문장이 <u>아닌</u> 것은?

① The email is sent every day.

② The report is not finished yet.

③ The food was served at 6 p.m.

④ The baker is baking bread now.

⑤ The song is sung by the choir.

[3-5] 다음 중 빈칸에 들어갈 말로 가장 적절한 것을 고르시오.

3

The letters __________ by the postman.

① deliver

② delivered

③ will deliver

④ are delivered

⑤ are delivering

4

The office __________ every night by the janitor.

① cleans

② cleaned

③ is cleaned

④ is cleaning

⑤ has cleaned

5

The meeting __________ last Friday by the members.

① attends

② is attended

③ was attended

④ is attending

⑤ was attending

[6-7] 다음 중 어법상 <u>틀린</u> 것을 고르시오.

6

① The reports submit weekly.

② My friends read the book.

③ The meeting is held every day.

④ The supplies are ordered by her.

⑤ The song was recorded yesterday.

① The keys belonged to the office.
② The situation is become serious.
③ The class was finished on time.
④ My phone was repaired last week.
⑤ The game is played on Mondays.

[8-9] **다음 문장을 수동태로 바르게 바꾼 것을 고르시오.**

8

The clerk is folding the clothes.

① The clerk is folded by the clothes.
② The clothes are folded by the clerk.
③ The clothes were folded by the clerk.
④ The clothes are being folded by the clerk.
⑤ The clothes were being folded by the clerk.

9

He will serve the food soon.

① The food is served soon by him.
② The food is serving soon by him.
③ The food will be served soon by him.
④ The food will be serving soon by him.
⑤ The food is going to serve soon by him.

[10-11] **다음 우리말에 맞도록 괄호 안의 단어를 이용하여 빈칸에 알맞은 말을 쓰시오.**

10

그 장난감은 내 남동생에게 주어졌다. (give)

→ The toy ____________ ____________ to my brother.

11

그 문자가 선생님에 의해 읽혀지고 있다. (read)

→ The message ____________ ____________ ____________ by the teacher.

[12-13] **다음 빈칸에 공통으로 들어갈 말로 가장 적절한 것을 고르시오.**

12

- The bottle is filled ______ water.
- They are satisfied ______ the new teacher.

① in   ② of
③ from   ④ with
⑤ at

13

- They were surprised _______ the news of the school closing.
- The meeting is held _______ the conference room.

① on
② at
③ of
④ to
⑤ for

14 다음 문장에서 어법상 틀린 곳을 바르게 고치시오.

> Was the decision making by the board members?

___________ → ___________

[15-16] 다음 대화의 빈칸에 들어갈 말이 바르게 짝지어진 것은?

15

A: _______ the paper printed daily?
B: Yes, the paper should _________ daily.

① Is - be printed
② Is - is printed
③ Do - be printed
④ Was - are printed
⑤ Was - be printing

16

A: Were the windows _______ in the morning?
B: No, the windows ___________.

① opened - were opened
② opened - be not opened
③ opening - were not opened
④ opening - not were opened
⑤ opened - were not opened

[17-18] 다음 대화의 빈칸에 들어갈 알맞은 말을 네 단어로 쓰시오.

17

A: _______________ during working hours?
B: Yes, the work is done during working hours.

→ _______________________

18

A: _______________ to all students?
B: No, the rules are not known to all students.

→ _______________________

19

그 주스는 신선한 오렌지로 만들어진다.
(made / the juice / from / fresh oranges / is / .)

→ ______________________________

20

이 문은 비행 중에 열려서는 안 된다.
(should / this door / not / opened / be / during the flight / .)

→ ______________________________

21 다음 두 문장을 한 문장으로 바꿔 쓸 때 빈칸에 알맞은 말을 쓰시오.

The chef prepares delicious meals every day. He uses fresh ingredients.

Delicious meals ______________ ______________ ______________ the chef every day with fresh ingredients.

[22-23] 다음 글을 읽고 물음에 답하시오.

The teacher explains the lesson to the students every day. Homework ⓐis assigned at the end of the lesson. Questions ⓑanswered after class. The homework ⓒis collected ⓓby the teacher the next day and ⓔchecked thoroughly.

22 위 글의 밑줄 친 문장을 수동태로 바꿔 쓰시오.

→ ______________________________

23 위 글의 밑줄 친 부분 중 어법상 틀린 것은?
① ⓐ   ② ⓑ   ③ ⓒ   ④ ⓓ   ⑤ ⓔ

혼공 중학 영문법 마스터

정답

CHAPTER 1
문장의 형식 1

혼공개념 pp. 8–9

A 1 He <u>sleeps</u> at night.
2 She <u>runs</u> in the morning.
3 They <u>swim</u> in the pool.

B 1 happy　2 easy　3 sweet

C 1 He has a car. (○)
2 We need some help. (○)

D 1 to　2 about

혼공연습 pp. 10–11

A 1 The baby <u>cried</u>.
2 Birds <u>fly</u> in the sky.
3 The kids <u>laugh</u> together.
4 The stars <u>twinkle</u> at night.
5 She <u>walks</u> to school.
6 The phone <u>rang</u> for a long time.
7 The sun <u>rises</u> in the east.
8 The bus <u>arrived</u> late today.

B 1 sad　2 looks　3 fresh　4 salty
5 sounds　6 feels　7 soft　8 perfect

C 1 writes　2 buys　3 open　4 clean　5 visit

D 1 to　2 for　3 with　4 to　5 for

혼공실전 1 pp. 12–15

A 1 It <u>rains</u>.
2 Cats <u>jump</u>.
3 Water <u>flows</u>.
4 The sun <u>sets</u>.
5 Fish <u>swim</u>.
6 The clock <u>ticks</u>.
7 The bell <u>rings</u>.
8 The car <u>stops</u>.
9 The wind <u>blows</u>.
10 The flower <u>blooms</u>.
11 Birds <u>sing</u> on the tree.
12 Noel <u>jogs</u> every morning.
13 They <u>exercise</u> in the evening.
14 The store <u>opens</u> at 9 a.m.
15 He <u>dances</u> all night.
16 He <u>left</u> in the morning.
17 She <u>stayed</u> with her friends.
18 She <u>moved</u> slowly.
19 They <u>arrived</u> safely.
20 The sun <u>shines</u> brightly.

B 1 looks　2 looks　3 sounds　4 sounds
5 peaceful　6 clear　7 strong　8 bad
9 strange　10 delicious　11 terrible
12 sweet　13 nice　14 sour　15 spicy
16 loose　17 hot　18 uncomfortable
19 nervous　20 important

C 1 angry　2 famous　3 rich　4 heavy
5 dark　6 warm　7 strong　8 weak
9 cold　10 soft　11 red　12 sour
13 clear　14 fresh　15 calm　16 healthy
17 wet　18 happy　19 quiet　20 honest

D 1 for　2 for　3 to　4 to　5 about　6 with
7 for　8 on　9 on　10 for

혼공실전 2 pp. 16–19

A 1 work　2 sleep　3 moves　4 dances
5 walks　6 sing　7 sets　8 stops　9 runs
10 swims　11 laugh　12 arrives

B 1 looks　2 smells　3 tastes　4 feels
5 sounds　6 looks　7 tastes　8 smells
9 smell　10 feels　11 looks　12 sounds

C 1 The water looks clear.
2 The baby looks sleepy.
3 The blanket feels warm.
4 The plan sounds great.
5 The chocolate tastes sweet.

6 The library looks quiet.

7 His face turned red.

8 I stayed awake all night.

9 We need to keep healthy.

10 The milk went bad.

11 The leaves turned yellow.

12 He grew strong after exercise.

13 The sky turned gray before the rain.

14 The room stayed warm all night.

15 She became nervous before the interview.

D 1 He listens to my advice.

2 She talks to her parents.

3 This eraser belongs to me.

4 He waited for the bus for 10 minutes.

5 She asked for some help.

6 I am looking for my textbook.

7 He paid for the snacks at the store.

8 She didn't agree with the new rules.

9 She relies on the internet for information.

10 She is focusing on her essay.

11 They laughed at the funny joke.

12 She participated in the group study.

13 She cares for her little brother after school.

14 You should deal with your stress.

15 They insist on their opinion.

혼공실전 3

pp. 20-23

1 ① 2 ③ 3 ④ 4 ⑤ 5 cold 6 smells
7 ③ 8 ④ 9 ④ 10 ② 11 ⑤ 12 ⑤

나는 아침에 버스를 기다렸다. 버스에서, 나는 내 계획에 대해 생각했다. 학교에서, 나는 친구들과 숙제에 대해 이야기했다. 수업 시간에는, 수업에 집중했다. 방과 후, 내 친구와 나는 카페를 찾았다. 나는 내 커피값을 지불했고, 친구의 재미있는 이야기를 들으며 웃었다.

13 warmly → warm   14 perfectly → perfect

15 ③   16 Wash your hands and stay healthy.

17 The shop will remain open until tomorrow.

18 ④   19 with   20 on

21 participate → participate in   22 ①

23 ⑤

내 친구와 나는 공원에 갔다. 꽃들은 아주 좋은 향기가 났다. 호수는 햇빛 아래에서 아주 평화로워 보였다. 우리는 벤치에 앉았다. 벤치는 따뜻하고 편안하게 느껴졌다. 우리 주변에 있는 모든 것이 잔잔하고 우리의 마음을 편안하게 하는 것 같았다. 얼굴에 스치는 산들바람이 시원하게 느껴졌다.

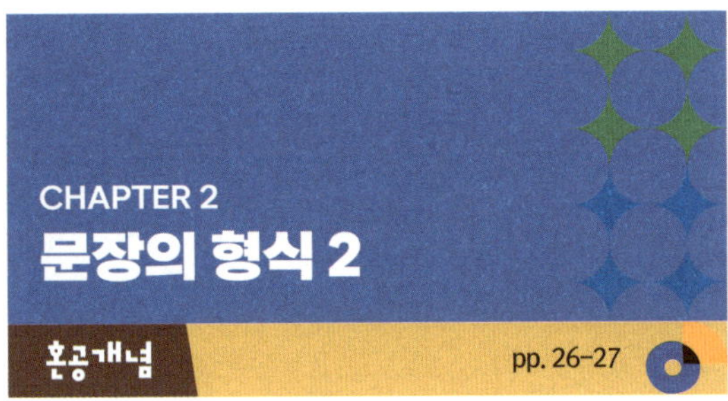

CHAPTER 2
문장의 형식 2

A 1 I gave <u>him</u> a book.
   2 He showed <u>us</u> his new car.
   3 My mom made <u>me</u> a sandwich.

B 1 to   2 for   3 of

C 1 ○   2 X   3 X

D 1 prepare   2 fly

A 1 me   2 her   3 him   4 us   5 them
   6 you   7 her   8 him

B 1 to   2 to   3 for   4 for   5 to   6 for
   7 for   8 of

C 1 named   2 him   3 warm   4 dark
   5 to study   6 to help us

D 1 clean   2 play   3 practice
   4 climb[climbing]   5 bark[barking]

A 1 gave   2 told   3 showed   4 sent
   5 cooked   6 bought   7 lent   8 made
   9 offered   10 them   11 you   12 her
   13 him   14 me   15 them   16 us   17 her
   18 them   19 us   20 him

B 1 to   2 to   3 to   4 for   5 to   6 for
   7 for   8 to   9 to   10 of   11 for   12 for
   13 to   14 to   15 of   16 for   17 for
   18 for   19 to   20 to

C 1 called   2 named   3 made   4 found
   5 kept   6 allowed   7 told   8 advised
   9 encouraged   10 ordered   11 found
   12 made   13 asked   14 wanted
   15 kept   16 made   17 found   18 made
   19 ordered   20 enabled

D 1 go   2 sing   3 clean   4 play   5 drawing
   6 wag   7 play   8 leave   9 blow   10 run

A 1 gave   2 bought   3 asked   4 sent
   5 lent   6 showed   7 read   8 brought
   9 offered   10 sent   11 gave   12 made

B 1 to   2 to   3 for   4 to   5 for   6 to   7 to
   8 to   9 for   10 of   11 to   12 to

C 1 She named her doll Lucy.
   2 He made the soup tasty.
   3 We kept the door open.
   4 We want her to join the team.
   5 They kept the baby quiet.
   6 We made the house warm.
   7 People called the invention a success.
   8 I asked him to open the window.
   9 They ordered the soldiers to move forward.
   10 I advised her to take a break.
   11 The teacher told us to write again.
   12 She allowed me to go to the party.
   13 We encouraged the children to play outside.
   14 She ordered him to finish the project.
   15 I found this city very beautiful.

D 1 We saw a cat sleep.
   2 The movie made us cry.
   3 The teacher saw us write the answers.
   4 The coach let us take a short break.
   5 We felt the car move.
   6 She watched her brother play soccer.
   7 I had my friend study English.
   8 The rain made us stay inside.
   9 I heard my sister sing in her room.
   10 We saw the bus leave the station.
   11 She let her friend borrow her book.

12 I heard someone knock on the door.

13 We watched her reading a book.

14 The manager had us arrange the chairs.

15 We watched the children play in the park.

1 ③   2 ⑤   3 ②   4 ①   5 ④   6 ③
7 ④   8 introduce   9 write   10 to
11 ④   12 ③

나는 어제 바빴다. 나는 친구에게 생일 선물로 책을 주었다. 그러고 나서, 동생에게 시험 볼 때 쓸 펜을 사주었다. 점심시간에는, 반 친구들에게 재미있는 이야기를 해 주었다. 후에, 여동생이 배고파해서 간식을 만들어 주었다. 저녁에는, 이웃에게 쿠키를 제공했다.

13 dancing → dance   14 learn → to learn

15 perfectly → perfect   16 ①   17 ⑤

18 to borrow   19 ①   20 ③

21 The doctor made me rest for a few days.

22 My son saw them helping an elderly man.

23 ②

한 농부가 가족과 함께 작은 마을에 살고 있었다. 어느 날, 그의 가족은 음식이 충분하지 않았다. 그는 가족이 더 많은 음식을 먹기를 원했다. 그는 자녀들에게 땅을 파고 씨앗을 심는 것을 도와달라고 요청했다. 농부는 동물들이 오래된 풀을 먹게 했다. 그는 그들의 노력이 식물이 자라게 할 것이라고 믿었다. 곧, 들판은 식량으로 가득 차게 되었고, 그의 가족은 행복했다.

CHAPTER 3
형용사와 부사

A 1 I have a <u>new</u> phone.
  2 The sky is <u>cloudy</u>.
  3 She gave me something <u>good</u>.

B 1 many   2 a few   3 little

C 1 We danced <u>happily</u>.
  2 <u>Clearly</u>, we made a mistake.
  3 The internet is <u>too</u> slow.

D 1 always likes   2 well

A 1 The coffee is <u>hot</u>.
  2 I want a <u>new</u> book.
  3 Her voice is <u>soft</u>.
  4 He likes a <u>small</u> dog.
  5 This dress is <u>expensive</u>.
  6 She has a <u>big</u> bag.
  7 We saw a <u>beautiful</u> bird.
  8 He works with <u>friendly</u> people.

B 1 many   2 much   3 a lot of   4 much
  5 a few   6 a little   7 Few   8 few

C 1 slowly   2 hard   3 loudly   4 clearly
  5 deeply

D 1 always   2 usually   3 sometimes   4 hardly
  5 never

A 1 colorful   2 noisy   3 healthy   4 beautiful
  5 readable   6 energetic   7 creative
  8 dangerous   9 famous   10 active
  11 comfortable   12 careful   13 peaceful

14 movable 15 helpful 16 effective
17 impressive 18 scientific 19 hopeful
20 humorous

B 1 Many 2 a few 3 a lot of 4 Few
5 a few 6 little 7 Many 8 little
9 a lot of 10 much 11 much 12 few
13 a little 14 few 15 little 16 Few
17 much 18 a lot of 19 Few 20 Little

C 1 slowly 2 easily 3 powerfully 4 really
5 rudely 6 fast 7 loudly 8 high
9 quickly 10 carefully 11 hard 12 well
13 smoothly 14 quietly 15 Luckily
16 clearly 17 Sadly 18 correctly
19 happily 20 Fortunately

D 1 always exercises 2 usually go
3 rarely watches 4 sometimes play
5 usually walks 6 never use 7 I'm never
8 is often 9 is always 10 is sometimes

혼공실전 ㄹ　　　　pp. 52–55

A 1 happy 2 beautiful 3 peaceful 4 easy
5 powerful 6 helpful 7 creative
8 comfortable 9 healthy 10 famous
11 dangerous 12 friendly

B 1 loudly 2 high 3 safely 4 warmly
5 late 6 near 7 recently 8 hard
9 clearly 10 really 11 brightly
12 naturally

C 1 She bought a few apples.
2 He poured a little water into the glass.
3 We took a few photos.
4 Few people solve the problems.
5 We will stay a few more minutes.
6 She needs a little rest after work.
7 He has little confidence.
8 He has little energy after school.
9 She made a few phone calls.
10 He made few mistakes on his test.

11 I need a few pens for my class.
12 He knows few songs.
13 There are a few buses running at night.
14 I have few opportunities to speak English.
15 We have a little bread for sandwiches.

D 1 We always have breakfast.
2 They usually take the bus.
3 I rarely see my old friends.
4 I hardly eat sweets.
5 We often go camping.
6 We rarely go to the countryside.
7 She sometimes wears bright colors.
8 She usually drinks tea.
9 They rarely complain about anything.
10 I often listen to a podcast.
11 He usually baked cookies for his
   neighbors.
12 He never goes out without his phone.
13 We hardly travel during the winter.
14 She sometimes borrows books from the
   library.
15 My mom always makes my favorite dish.

혼공실전 ㅋ　　　　pp. 56–59

1 ④ 2 ③ 3 ④ 4 ④ 5 ① 6 ②
7 ⑤ 8 a few 9 never 10 too 11 ①
12 ③

그날은 Sam에게 행복한 날이었다. 그는 일찍 일어나 밝게 미소 지었다. 태양이 따뜻하게 빛나며 그를 기분 좋게 했다. Sam은 맛있는 아침을 빨리 먹었다. 그 후, 그는 친구들을 만나러 신나게 달려갔다. 그들은 하루 종일 행복하게 놀았다.

13 regular → regularly
14 Honest → Honestly
15 many → much
16 ⑤ 17 ⑤ 18 loudly 19 ⑤ 20 ①
21 She is never late for school.
22 They hardly study for their exams. 23 ④

내 여동생은 아침에 일찍 일어난다. 그녀는 방을 나서기 전에 항상 침대를 정리한다. 아침 식사 후, 그녀는 자주 책을 읽거나 조용히 공부한다. 만약 날씨가 좋으면, 그녀는 때때로 공원에서 산책을 한다. 그녀는 독서를 더 좋아하기 때문에 저녁에 TV를 거의 보지 않는다. 잠자리에 들기 전에, 그녀는 보통 차 한 잔을 마신다.

CHAPTER 4
전치사

 pp. 62-63 

A 1 This gift is <u>for</u> you.
　2 The cat ran <u>to</u> the door.
　3 I played soccer <u>with</u> my friends

B 1 in　2 on　3 under

C 1 in　2 from　3 for

D 1 with　2 with　3 from

 pp. 64-65

A 1 He is <u>in</u> the room.
　2 The book is <u>on</u> the desk.
　3 We met <u>at</u> the bus stop.
　4 The cat is <u>under</u> the chair.
　5 The tree is <u>between</u> two houses.
　6 The store closes <u>at</u> 7 p.m.
　7 She talks <u>about</u> her family.
　8 He eats lunch <u>with</u> his mom.

B 1 in　2 at　3 on　4 in　5 near
　6 between　7 above　8 behind

C 1 in　2 on　3 at　4 on　5 at

D 1 with　2 for　3 of　4 from　5 for

 pp. 66-69 

A 1 of　2 for　3 about　4 for　5 of　6 to
　7 of　8 about　9 to　10 about　11 to
　12 of　13 to　14 with　15 of　16 of
　17 about　18 with　19 from　20 for

B 1 in　2 at　3 in　4 on　5 on　6 in
　7 above　8 at　9 in　10 behind
　11 in front of　12 under　13 at

14 behind 15 on 16 on 17 under
18 at 19 in front of 20 between

C 1 at 2 at 3 in 4 toward 5 in 6 up
7 in 8 up 9 during 10 on 11 for
12 during 13 on 14 for 15 in 16 for
17 on 18 toward 19 for 20 in

D 1 with 2 with 3 for 4 for 5 of 6 of
7 from 8 with 9 from 10 for

 pp. 70-73

A 1 on 2 under 3 about 4 near
5 behind 6 in front of 7 in 8 about
9 above 10 from 11 under 12 between

B 1 in 2 at 3 on 4 before 5 after 6 on
7 for 8 up 9 during 10 from 11 in
12 for

C 1 on the bench 2 under the tree
3 on March 24th 4 in the 1990s
5 for two hours 6 of the house
7 from different countries
8 near my house 9 with his friends
10 behind my apartment
11 in front of the shopping mall
12 during the vacation 13 after lunch
14 before midnight 15 at noon

D 1 I replace the batteries with new ones.
2 If you mix blue with yellow, you get green.
3 They provided us with useful information.
4 He thanked her for her kindness.
5 She informed me of the meeting time.
6 I stopped him from making a big mistake.
7 He mistook me for my older brother.
8 The mask keeps me from breathing in dust.
9 She criticized her friend for being late.
10 They robbed the bank of five million dollars.
11 The fans blamed the coach for the
team's loss.
12 The storm deprived the village of
electricity.

13 The teacher prohibited us from talking
during the test.
14 I prevent my dog from running into the
street.
15 The store compensated me for the
damaged product.

 pp. 74-77 

1 ④ 2 ① 3 ③ 4 ③ 5 ③ 6 ②
7 ② 8 ② 9 ④ 10 ⑤ 11 ④ 12 ④

Jenny는 부엌으로 걸어가서 차를 준비했다. 그리고 소파에 앉아 책을 읽었다. 그녀의 고양이는 기뻐서 그녀의 무릎 위로 뛰어올랐다. 그녀는 책을 테이블 위에 놓고 일어섰다. 그리고, 그녀는 산책을 하기 위해 밖으로 나갔다.

13 ⑤ 14 ③ 15 for 16 from 17 of
18 ② 19 at → of 20 on → of
21 to → from 22 ③ 23 ②

Emma는 그녀의 낡은 휴대폰을 새로운 것으로 교체하고 싶었다. 그녀의 친구는 그녀에게 가게에서 진행 중인 큰 할인 행사에 대해 알려 주었다. 그녀는 친구에게 도움을 주어 고맙다고 했다. 가게에서, 그녀는 한 손님을 직원으로 착각할 뻔했다. 그녀는 새 휴대폰을 구입하고 만족감을 느꼈다.

CHAPTER 5
현재완료

  pp. 80–81

A 1 went 2 has gone

B 1 I haven't done it. (○)

  2 Has he finished it? (○)

C 1 그녀는 이미 그 일을 시작했다.

  2 그는 파리에 몇 번 방문한 적이 있다.

D 1 나는 여기에서 5년 동안 살고 있다.

  2 나는 열쇠를 잃어버린 상태이다.

혼공연습 pp. 82–83

A 1 I have joined a contest.

  2 We have done the work.

  3 He has played basketball.

  4 I haven't seen that movie.

  5 He has returned my book.

  6 I have answered all the questions.

  7 We have visited a historical place.

  8 She has studied English since last year.

B 1 Have 2 Has 3 tried 4 haven't

  5 been 6 stayed 7 met 8 have

C 1 have, read 2 has, eaten 3 have, arrived

  4 has been 5 have seen 6 have heard

D 1 have never met 2 have never sung

  3 has never flown 4 Have, done

  5 Have, cooked 6 Has, tried

혼공실전 1 pp. 84–87

A 1 ○ 2 X 3 ○ 4 X 5 ○ 6 ○ 7 X

  8 ○ 9 ○ 10 ○ 11 X 12 ○ 13 ○

  14 X 15 X 16 X 17 X 18 ○ 19 ○

  20 X

B 1 경험 2 완료 3 경험 4 완료 5 경험

  6 완료 7 계속 8 완료 9 계속 10 완료

  11 경험 12 계속 13 경험 14 완료

  15 계속 16 완료 17 경험 18 결과

  19 계속 20 결과

C 1 He has played the piano.

  2 I have bought a new jacket.

  3 We have run in a race.

  4 I have not[haven't] packed my bag.

  5 We have not[haven't] decided to go.

  6 She has not[hasn't] closed the door.

  7 We have never stayed in a hotel.

  8 She has never been to a concert.

  9 They have never seen a tiger.

  10 Has she gone camping?

  11 Have you been to the mountains?

  12 Have you ever written a poem?

  13 Has he ever tried skydiving?

  14 Have you ever lived in another country?

  15 Have you ever been to a music festival?

D 1 read, hasn't

  2 Has, has

  3 Did, didn't

  4 run, have

  5 Do, don't

  6 Has, hasn't

  7 spoken, hasn't

  8 before, haven't

  9 been, have

  10 changed, hasn't

혼공실전 2 pp. 88–91

A 1 have been 2 have, made 3 has already

  4 have seen[watched] 5 studied, for

  6 has, since 7 have been 8 have, read

  9 has written 10 has drawn

  11 have visited 12 have played

B 1 not cleaned 2 have never

3 haven't discussed 4 haven't solved
5 never eaten 6 haven't started
7 Has, called[phoned] 8 already changed
9 ever eaten[tried] 10 Has, left
11 Have, ever 12 Has, already

C 1 (○) 2 (X) broke → broken
3 (X) has → have 4 (X) saw → seen
5 (○) 6 (X) plan → planned 7 (○)
8 (X) took → taken
9 (X) Have → Has 10 (○)
11 (X) don't have → have not[haven't]
12 (X) experience → experienced 13 (○)
14 (○) 15 (X) ago → before

D 1 I have opened the window.
2 Amy has cooked dinner.
3 He has packed his bag.
4 My son has done his chores.
5 They have arrived at the park.
6 She has moved to a new house.
7 We have practiced English for 3 years.
8 I have never had a pet.
9 We have never gone on a picnic.
10 She has not tasted the new cookies.
11 Have they paid the bill?
12 Has he learned the skills?
13 Has she gone to the gym?
14 Have you heard of that singer?
15 Have your sons built a sandcastle?

혼공실전 3
pp. 92-95

1 ② 2 ⑤ 3 ③ 4 ① 5 ③
6 have seen 7 not[never] played 8 ④
9 ④ 10 ③ 11 ④ 12 ②

나는 많은 나라를 여행한 적이 있다. 작년에는 이탈리아에 가서 2주 동안 머물렀다. 나는 언제나 로마 방문을 꿈꿔 왔는데, 드디어 그 꿈을 이루었다. 그 여행은 정말 기억에 남았고, 곧 더 많은 곳을 탐험하고 싶다.

13 hear → heard 14 Have → Has 15 ⑤
16 They have not left yet.

17 I have never been late for school. 18 ③
19 ago 20 before 21 after → since
22 ②, ⑤ 23 ⑤

나는 지난 주말에 할머니, 할아버지 댁에 갔다. 우리는 함께 즐거운 시간을 보냈다. 나는 사촌들과 게임을 하고, 공원에서 산책을 했다. 그때 이후, 할머니, 할아버지와 전화 통화를 몇 번 했다. 다음 달에 다시 할머니, 할아버지 댁에 가기로 계획을 세웠다.

CHAPTER 6
to 부정사

혼공개념   pp. 98–99

A 1 To play   2 to go

B 1 to fix   2 how to

C 1 He has a letter to read. (○)
   2 We need someone to talk with. (○)

D 1 ⓒ   2 ⓐ   3 ⓑ

혼공연습   pp. 100–101

A 1 I need <u>to buy</u> groceries.
   2 We love <u>to watch</u> movies.
   3 X
   4 She decided <u>to start</u> a new project.
   5 <u>To eat</u> vegetables is good for health.
   6 <u>To run</u> every day keeps you healthy.
   7 X
   8 <u>To read</u> books expands your knowledge.

B 1 to write   2 to plan   3 increase
   4 to respect   5 to eat   6 to solve
   7 How   8 what

C 1 a car to drive   2 a book to study
   3 something to eat   4 is to join
   5 is to start   6 are to finish

D 1 따뜻하게 유지하기 위해
   2 결국 시험에 떨어졌다
   3 그 소식을[뉴스를] 듣게 되어
   4 그 상자를 드는 것을 보니
   5 토요일이라는 것을 깨달았다

혼공실전 1   pp. 102–105

A 1 △   2 ○   3 ○   4 △   5 ○   6 ○   7 △
   8 △   9 ○   10 △   11 ○   12 △   13 △

14 △   15 △   16 ○   17 △   18 ○   19 △
20 ○

B 1 그 기차는 정오에 떠날 예정이다.
   2 그 콘서트는 30분 후에 시작할 예정이다.
   3 그 비행기는 오후 6시에 떠날 예정이다.
   4 그 영화는 다음 주에 개봉할 예정이다.
   5 그 행사는 본관에서 진행될 예정이다.
   6 그들은 업무 후에 사무실을 청소해야 한다.
   7 그는 반드시 회의에 참석해야 한다.
   8 우리는 지시 사항을 주의하여 따라야 한다.
   9 당신은 면접을[인터뷰를] 위해 정시에 도착해야
     한다.
   10 그 직원은 마감일까지 양식을 제출해야 한다.
   11 그녀는 자기 분야에서 지도자가 될 운명이다.
   12 그는 유명한 음악가가 될 운명이다.
   13 우리는 기차를 타려면 지금 떠나야 한다.
   14 그녀가 의사가 되려면 더 열심히 공부해야 한다.

C 1 to call   2 to be   3 to think   4 to keep
   5 to find   6 to avoid   7 to teach
   8 to visit   9 to get   10 to lose
   11 to achieve   12 to save   13 to have
   14 to spend   15 to see   16 to study
   17 to wrap   18 to go with   19 to write on
   20 to sit on

D 1 work on, to
   2 to begin, is to
   3 to sign, to
   4 to, to
   5 to pay, pay
   6 write on, for
   7 is, defeat
   8 where to, find
   9 bake, to make
   10 use, install

혼공실전 2   pp. 106–109

A 1 to learn   2 is to reduce   3 To write
   4 is to open   5 to become   6 To speak
   7 to visit   8 is to take   9 To help

10 To travel   11 To learn   12 was to clean

B 1 What to   2 where to   3 how to
4 What to   5 What to   6 when to
7 where to   8 when to   9 who to
10 who to   11 where to   12 How to

C 1 I found a place to stay.
2 I need a website to visit.
   [I need to visit a website.]
3 She has a chair to sit on.
4 To be on time is a good habit.
5 To love yourself is important.
6 They want to go to the beach.
7 I hope to finish the task.
8 We plan to improve our website.
9 She decided to move to a new city.
10 To take risks can bring rewards.
11 Her idea is to start a new business.
12 To trust others builds strong bonds.
13 His purpose is to improve his health.
14 To focus on your work improves results.
15 Their plan is to launch a new product.

D 1 I bought something to write with.
2 I hired someone to clean the house.
3 They found someone to join their team.
4 They have something to give you.
5 He was excited to start his new job.
6 He went to the store to buy groceries.
7 They woke up early to catch the train.
8 He trained every day to win the
   championship.
9 What to learn next is your decision.
10 I'm not sure where to eat for lunch.
11 Tell me what to buy for the picnic.
12 We heard what to bring to the event.
13 I have no idea what to study for the exam.
14 Do you know how to play chess?
15 Can you show me how to make a website?

혼공실전 3   pp. 110-113

1 ④   2 ④   3 ①   4 ⑤   5 To enjoy
6 is to   7 ⑤   8 ④   9 ①   10 ④   11 ④
12 ③   13 shares → to share
14 success → succeed   15 ②   16 ⑤
17 The class is to start at 10 o'clock.
18 She must be brave to go there alone.
19 ①   20 in   21 about
22 A: what → how   B: for → to   23 ③

내 꿈은 전문 가수가 되는 것이다. 나에게는 음악과 관련된 것들을 탐구하고자 하는 열정이 있다. 나는 목소리를 더 좋게 만들기 위해 꾸준히 연습한다. 그리고 나의 여정을 이끌어 줄 멘토를 찾았다. 공연을 거듭할 때마다, 나는 자신감이 생긴다. 언젠가, 나처럼 음악을 사랑하는 사람들을 돕고 싶다.

CHAPTER 7
to 부정사와 동명사

A 1 enough   2 too

B 1 to travel   2 to wait   3 to use

C 1 Swimming   2 teaching

D 1 I enjoy singing songs. (○)
   2 He gave up playing soccer. (○)

A 1 about   2 about   3 too   4 enough
   5 too   6 order   7 order   8 not

B 1 to leave   2 call   3 to study   4 to go
   5 to travel   6 to learn   7 to hear

C 1 swimming   2 Writing   3 singing
   4 Reading   5 painting

D 1 mind   2 practices   3 keeps   4 finished
   5 quit

A 1 about   2 not   3 not   4 about   5 too
   6 enough   7 too   8 about   9 enough
   10 about   11 not   12 not   13 order
   14 too   15 enough   16 order   17 too
   18 order   19 enough

B 1 to try   2 working   3 working
   4 traveling   5 to meet   6 writing
   7 to get   8 to finish   9 to learn
   10 fishing   11 to be   12 to be
   13 to improve   14 to learn   15 to join
   16 to use   17 to visit   18 to improve
   19 stealing   20 watching

C 1 to live   2 breaking   3 going   4 to join
   5 to meet   6 cheating   7 to quit
   8 leaving   9 to be   10 to live
   11 to submit   12 to speak   13 opening
   14 to solve   15 trying   16 to leave
   17 to finish   18 to perform   19 to be
   20 to take

D 1 to fix, helping
   2 reading, to start
   3 turning, to switch
   4 to go, to save
   5 to stop, having
   6 checking, to hear
   7 to visit, to see
   8 to bake, baking
   9 learning, practicing
   10 breaking, to apologize

A 1 is about to   2 hot enough to
   3 too, to buy   4 not to   5 enough to
   6 too old to   7 too sick to   8 is about to
   9 in order to   10 enough to   11 not to be
   12 in order to

B 1 to start   2 eating   3 cooking   4 to join
   5 to stop   6 to speak   7 taking   8 waiting
   9 drawing   10 to know   11 to attend
   12 to work

C 1 Playing games is exciting.
   2 Painting is her passion.
   3 Cooking is a useful skill.
   4 Singing makes me happy.
   5 Jogging keeps you healthy.
   6 I consider quitting my job.
   7 She hates doing homework.
   8 Dancing is my favorite hobby.
   9 Fishing at the lake is very relaxing.
   10 My favorite activity is reading.
   11 Their main interest is cooking.

12 Traveling broadens your mind.

13 My father loves cooking dinner.

14 Her specialty is playing the violin.

15 Setting his objective is important.

D 1 He delayed taking the exam.

2 She denied taking the money.

3 I admitted lying to my friend.

4 We put off deciding the menu.

5 She quit looking for a new job.

6 I avoid going to crowded places.

7 Polar bears enjoy swimming in the ocean.

8 We admitted making a mistake.

9 I keep thinking about the decision.

10 He enjoys hiking in the mountains.

11 He considered changing his career.

12 I don't mind cooking dinner tonight.

13 He practices running every morning.

14 We finished doing the homework.

15 She didn't give up studying math.

혼공실전 ㅋ pp. 128–131

1 ④ 2 ④, ⑤ 3 ③ 4 ② 5 ③ 6 about
7 not to 8 too 9 enough 10 ① 11 ⑤
12 ② 13 ①, ④ 14 ① 15 ③
16 enjoy → to enjoy 17 see → to see
18 Jimmy hates waiting[to wait] in long lines.
19 They practice playing soccer every evening.
20 living → to live 21 too spicy to eat
22 hope, to travel 23 ⑤

Shannon은 매일 그녀의 친구와 이야기하곤 했다. 어느 날, 그 친구가 그녀에게 거짓말을 했고, Shannon은 그녀를 그만 믿기로 결심했다. 그래서, 그녀는 그 친구와 이야기하는 것을 그만두었다. 그녀는 정직한 친구들을 찾고 싶었다. 그녀는 새로운 사람들을 만나는 것을 즐겼다. 이제, 그녀는 새로운 정직한 친구들이 있어 행복하다.

CHAPTER 8
수동태

혼공개념 pp. 134–135

A 1 is written 2 is built

B 1 is 2 was 3 be

C 1 The car is not washed by him. (○)
2 Is the box moved by the boy? (○)

D 1 as 2 at

혼공연습 pp. 136–137

A 1 △ 2 ○ 3 △ 4 △
5 ○ 6 ○ 7 ○ 8 △

B 1 was cut 2 was finished 3 was
4 will be 5 will be 6 was 7 are being
8 is being

C 1 is not done 2 is not supported
3 is not cleaned 4 Is, graded 5 Is, tested
6 Are, shipped

D 1 given to 2 filled with
3 surprised at 4 satisfied with
5 known to

혼공실전 1 pp. 138–141

A 1 X 2 ○ 3 ○ 4 X 5 X 6 X 7 ○
8 X 9 ○ 10 ○ 11 X 12 ○ 13 X
14 ○ 15 ○ 16 X 17 ○ 18 X 19 ○
20 X

B 1 is 2 will be 3 will be 4 is 5 are being
6 were 7 be 8 was 9 will be 10 be
11 is 12 reviewed 13 be delivered
14 are being 15 be written 16 were
17 being 18 was 19 is 20 was

C 1 started, is started
2 directed, directed
3 Was, didn't train
4 assigned, is assigned
5 Did, were not made
6 solve, was
7 given, wasn't
8 decorated, was
9 Were, were not
10 Were, were not ironed

D 1 of 2 from 3 with 4 as 5 by 6 in
7 to 8 to 9 with 10 as 11 at

혼공실전 ㄹ pp. 142-145

A 1 The room was painted
2 The meals are prepared
3 The invitation was sent
4 The questions are answered
5 Their mistakes are pointed
6 The homework is being checked
7 The project was completed
8 The reports will be prepared
9 The plans are being processed
10 The job was being done
11 The results will not be
12 The documents are not filed
13 The meeting wasn't planned
14 The files were not transferred
15 Is the room cleaned

B 1 Groceries were bought by her.
2 The thief was caught by the police.
3 A wrong turn was taken by them.
4 A new playground was built by them.
5 The answer to the question was found by him.
6 The movie was not[wasn't] loved by him.
7 The email was not[wasn't] written by her.
8 Books are not[aren't] sold by the convenience store.

C 1 She eats an apple.
2 We saw the movie.
3 She gives a gift to her friend.
4 They sold their house last year.
5 He calls his mother every evening.
6 They did not[didn't] help us.

D 1 is locked 2 is cleaned 3 is not served
4 was eaten 5 were called 6 was given
7 were not sent 8 was not helped
9 are being sorted 10 is being worked
11 was being discussed
12 was being renovated
13 was being written 14 Was, signed by
15 Are, being painted

E 1 She is not seen by anyone.
2 A sandwich is made by the chef.
3 Her keys were found by her.
4 He is interested in joining the football team.
5 The furniture is not made from wood.
6 A new car was bought by us.
7 The book was published in 2005.
8 The shoes were not sold last year.
9 The book was given to me by the teacher.
10 The task was being completed by the boss.
11 The customers are being served by the staff.
12 Was the package delivered yesterday?
13 Is the movie watched by a lot of people?
14 The exam results will be posted online.
15 The schedule should be followed by all members.

혼공실전 ㅋ pp. 146-149

1 ⑤ 2 ④ 3 ④ 4 ③ 5 ③ 6 ①
7 ② 8 ④ 9 ③ 10 was given
11 is being read 12 ④ 13 ②
14 making → made 15 ① 16 ⑤
17 Is the work done 18 Are the rules known
19 The juice is made from fresh oranges.

20 This door should not be opened during the flight.

21 are prepared by

22 The lesson is explained to the students every day by the teacher.[The lesson is explained to the students by the teacher every day.]

23 ②

선생님은 매일 학생들에게 수업 내용을 설명하신다. 수업이 끝날 때 숙제가 주어진다. 질문은 수업이 끝날 때쯤에 답변된다. 숙제는 다음 날 선생님에 의해 모아져 철저히 검사된다.

초판 1쇄 발행　2025년 6월 23일

지은이　허준석
편집　강지희 홍하늘
디자인　박새롬
마케팅　두잉글 사업본부

펴낸곳　혼공북스
출판등록　제2021-000288호
주소　04033 서울특별시 마포구 양화로 113, 4층(서교동, 순흥빌딩)
전자메일　team@hongong.co.kr

혼공북스는 ㈜혼공유니버스의 출판 브랜드입니다.

ISBN　979-11-984935-8-3　13740